REAL AND PERSONAL PROPERTY

UNDER QUEEN VICTORIA.

THE HISTORY OF THE LEGISLATION

CONCERNING

REAL AND PERSONAL PROPERTY

IN ENGLAND

DURING THE REIGN OF QUEEN VICTORIA

BY

J. E. R. DE VILLIERS, LL.M.

OF THE INNER TEMPLE;

FELLOW OF ST JOHN'S COLLEGE;
GEORGE LONG PRIZEMAN, CHANCELLOR'S GOLD MEDALLIST IN LAW,
AND WHEWELL INTERNATIONAL LAW SCHOLAR, CAMBRIDGE;
ADVOCATE OF THE SUPREME COURT OF THE CAPE OF GOOD HOPE.

(BEING THE YORKE PRIZE ESSAY FOR THE YEAR 1900)

LONDON
C. J. CLAY AND SONS
CAMBRIDGE UNIVERSITY PRESS WAREHOUSE
AVE MARIA LANE

1901

CAMBRIDGE
UNIVERSITY PRESS

University Printing House, Cambridge CB2 8BS, United Kingdom

Cambridge University Press is part of the University of Cambridge.

It furthers the University's mission by disseminating knowledge in the pursuit of
education, learning and research at the highest international levels of excellence.

www.cambridge.org
Information on this title: www.cambridge.org/9781316626191

© Cambridge University Press 1901

First published 1901
First paperback edition 2016

A catalogue record for this publication is available from the British Library

ISBN 978-1-316-62619-1 Paperback

DEDICATED

THE INIMITABLE

DUCHESKA.

"Nihil simul inventum est atque perfectum."

PREFACE.

THE writer of the following chapters has found it advisable not strictly to confine his attention to actually achieved legislation, but sometimes to deal with mere schemes and projects of historical importance. The law of Married Women's Property, on the other hand, has been altogether omitted, inasmuch as it has already formed the subject of two Yorke Prize Essays.

In the subjoined list are enumerated the principal authorities consulted; these and other authorities are separately referred to in footnotes. The writer may state, however, that by far the greatest part of his information has been obtained directly and laboriously from the Blue Books mentioned at the head of the list.

Reports of Royal Commissions and Select Committees, and the Evidence of witnesses examined by them.
Hansard's Parliamentary Debates.
The Law Reports.
James Humphreys on Real Property (1826).
John Miller on the Civil Law (1825).
Joshua Williams on the Transfer of Land (1862).

C. S. Kenny on Endowed Charities.

Joseph Kay's "Free Trade in Land."

Shaw Lefevre's "Agrarian Tenures."

Leone Levi's "History of British Commerce."

Sir F. Pollock's "Essays in Jurisprudence and Ethics."

Mill's "Political Economy" and Bentham's "Theory of Legislation."

Report adopted by Bar Committee 25 March 1886, drawn up by Messrs Davey, Q.C., Rigby, Q.C., M.P., Dunning, Byrne and Digby.

The Reports of the Real Property Commission are cited as "First Report" etc. Their full references are:—First Report, Parl. Pap. 1829, vol. x; Second Report, P. P. 1830, vol. xi; Third Report, P. P. 1831—2, vol. xxiii; Fourth Report, P. P. 1833, vol. xxii.

St John's College.
November, 1900.

CONTENTS.

	PAGE
INTRODUCTION	xi

CHAPTER I.

| LAND TRANSFER AND TITLE . . . . . . | 1 |

CHAPTER II.

| LAND TRANSFER AND TITLE (*continued*) . . . . | 29 |

CHAPTER III.

| TENURES AND THEIR INCIDENTS . . . . . | 77 |

CHAPTER IV.

| TESTAMENTS AND INTESTACY . . . . . . | 105 |

CHAPTER V.

| MONOPOLIES . . . . | 126 |

CHAPTER VI.

PAGE

COMMERCIAL LAW 161

CHAPTER VII.

DEBTS AND SECURITIES 189

INDEX 235

INTRODUCTION.

WHEN Queen Victoria ascended the throne, the first great burst of reform was spending its energies on the Law of Real Property. The reforming forces had slowly been accumulating. George the Third had reigned during a period of national optimism, the conviction that the law of England was both relatively and absolutely perfect not having been confined to Blackstone, "that eminent dealer in panegyric." The general complacency had been too great to be shaken even by Bentham, first of legal philosophers, whose vivid exposition of abuses and absurdities remained for many years unheeded.

The influences adverse to reform were indeed strong. There was the *vis inertiae* of conservatism, the veneration inspired by a body of law descending unrevised from the reign of Edward the First, and of a complexity so involved that even the Real Property Commissioners, unsurpassed in legal lore, confessed to a large measure of ignorance. As to the great body of legal practitioners, it might be said that they had no more than a fragmentary and empirical knowledge of the law. The law, again, was so permeated with abuses, that even

were a reformer forthcoming possessed of adequate
knowledge and destitute of the sentiment of veneration,
he would not have known on what particular mischief
to bestow his first attention, and by what principle to
limit his efforts; isolated reforms might worse confound
the confusion. The Courts both of law and of equity
had played their successive parts in the building of
the law, but their day was past. We shall find
numerous instances in which both Judges and Chan-
cellors confessed themselves beaten in an unequal
struggle against the stubborn iniquities which they
were compelled to administer. The time had come
for the third great formative agency of law, comprehensive legislation was urgently needed.

The wisdom of Bentham gradually spread downward.
In Parliament, Sir Samuel Romilly, Bentham's great
pupil, perseveringly applied the principles of his master
to the improvement of the law, more especially of the
Criminal law. On his tragic and premature death in
1818, he left behind him comprehensive and admirable
schemes for the reform of the law, many of which have
since been realized. His place was for an interval
taken by Sir James Mackintosh, a legal reformer
equally zealous, but less successful and less practical.
Out of Parliament, in the meantime, the condition of
the law, and particularly of the law of Real Property,
was receiving the earnest attention of a school of
jurists, enthusiastic, erudite, and filled with admiration
for Bentham. In 1825 appeared John Miller's *Inquiry
into the State of the Civil Law*. In 1826 James
Humphreys wrote his *Observations on the actual state
of the English Law of Real Property, with the outline*

of a Code. This admirable and effective work, to which the Real Property Commissioners acknowledged "a debt of gratitude," was described by Henry Brougham as an "honest, patient, and luminous discussion by one of the first conveyancers and lawyers this country could ever boast of[1]." In 1827 Sugden's *Letters to James Humphrey* concerning the improvement of the law of Real Property, were published.

On the 7th February 1828, Henry Brougham (soon to become Lord Brougham) delivered his memorable speech on the state of the law, a speech which will ever remain a landmark in the history of our legislation. For six hours he held the attention of Parliament while he perambulated the law of England, enumerating its principal defects and abuses[2]. Many rules of the Common Law were absurd and unjust *per se*, owing to the inevitable limitations and circumscriptions of judiciary law-making. Others had become so through the gradual and imperceptible evolution of everything else besides themselves during the many centuries since they had been first created. "Conditions had changed, the law had not"; the observation has a trite appearance, but it accounts for what would otherwise give cause for much reflection on the common-sense of our tribunals.

The most important consequence, for our purpose, of Brougham's great speech, was the appointment by Lord Chancellor Lyndhurst of a Royal Commission to consider the state of the law of real property. At the

---

[1] *Speech on Law Reform*, as separately edited, p. 4.

[2] Hansard, xviii. from p. 127.

head of the Commission was John Campbell, afterwards Lord Campbell and Lord Chancellor. Among those consulted by the Commissioners may be mentioned Bentham himself, and John Tyrrell, a lawyer, whose opinions and rescripts were separately published in 1829, to satisfy the eager demands of the profession. The radical reforms brought about by the Real Property Commissioners broke the ice and overcame once for all the resistances due to veneration and to ignorance. Thenceforth the improvement of the law went on by a process comparatively uninterrupted, if slow and gradual. Both as a parliamentary orator and as the head of the Law Amendment Society founded by him, Lord Brougham continued to be a successful law-reformer until his death in 1868. Each reform not only made the next reform more easy to bring about and more practicable to execute, but also threw into a more glaring relief the remaining defects of the law.

It is not easy to characterize generally the property-legislation of the Queen's reign. That it has been all in the way of improvement, goes almost without saying. Too often, however, the process has been fragmentary, halting, and overcautious. To some extent, this has been part of the price paid for the benefits of representative government ; to some extent it has been due to that dogmatic trait of English character, preferring to put its trust in well-worn institutions which have stood the test of time, which have grown and not been made. Both these influences have until recently acted with exaggerated force through the want of a trained legal body, such as that recommended by Bentham and Mill, entrusted with the form and detail of legislation.

Equally difficult is it to formulate the general principles pervading the vast department of legislation which we propose to consider. "The admitted functions of government," Mill has observed, "embrace a much wider field than can easily be included within the ring-fence of any restrictive definition[1]." The great principle of Utility, of the happiness of the political community and its posterity, though never totally lost to the view of our legislators, has during the last sixty years been more fully and more consciously applied to the business of making and changing laws. This movement or tendency may reasonably be ascribed to the growth of true democracy, the increasing enlightenment of the public, and, not least, to the guiding impulse of the irresistible truths of Bentham and Mill. In connection with the happiness of the political community, it is not proposed to discuss the relation of the legislator to the hierarchy of the pleasures constituting that happiness, further than by drawing the distinction that so far as the laws of *property* are concerned, utility or expediency usually means nothing more nor less than wealth. We shall have opportunities of finding that this is true of legislation concerning all sorts and conditions of proprietary rights. Wealth is everywhere aimed at, if not as an end, then at any rate as the means to other kinds or degrees of happiness. The exceptional cases in which proprietary legislation has aimed directly and immedi-

[1] *Political Economy*, Book v. ch. i.

ately at the happiness ulterior to wealth occur
principally in what is vaguely called "special legislation." Thus one of the main foundations of the law
of copyright arises out of the desirability of the moral,
literary and artistic instruction of the community; the
current of real property legislation, again, has lately
set towards the moral reconstruction of the agricultural
labourer; recent bankruptcy law, even in its strictly
proprietary aspect, proceeds upon the assumption that
the limits of State interference include the morality of
commerce. Other examples will occur in which moral
considerations obviously enter, but in very few cases
can the line be distinctly drawn; morality itself is
sometimes fostered as a means to the increase of
wealth.

The general identification of Expediency and Wealth
in proprietary legislation has given both prominence
and influence to the doctrines of Political Economy.
Wealth or property being the peculiar province both
of property-law and of political economy, it is natural
and almost inevitable that the one should react on the
other. This we shall find to have occurred in our own
legislation. Political economy has had many avenues
of influence, not only through the general dissemination
of economic knowledge, but also through the consul-
tation of eminent economists by Royal Commissions
and Select Committees, and the use of their opinions
in parliamentary discussion. The debate, for example,
on the Limited Partnership Bill of 1854 was little else
than a conflict between the authority of Mill on the
one hand, and of M'Culloch, the economic Blackstone,
on the other. As political economy has fluctuated and

reconsidered its positions, so has legislation. During the earlier half of the Queen's reign Individualism and *Laisser-faire* were in exclusive possession of the field. During the latter half of the reign a truer understanding of the limitations of those doctrines has resulted in not a few socialisms and in not a few legislative interferences with the freedom of contract. The chief examples will be found in the law concerning tenant-farmers and their landlords.

In the department of Real Property the legislation of the reign has been a not unsuccessful process of simplification. Land is indestructible, and its uses are infinite; it is the raw material of subsistence, of habitation, and of all manufacture and commerce. The law of land is proportionately and inevitably complex. The law of English land had been developed to a quite superfluous degree of complexity during the long period of elaboration preceding the nineteenth century. With personalty it has been otherwise. The law of personal property being of a later origin and therefore in itself more reasonable, the recent course of legislation has been, after the correction of sundry abuses, to complicate rather than to simplify that law. The progress of commerce, of invention, of manufactures, of associative industry, has every now and then necessitated the introduction or the development of some institution unknown or imperfectly known to the older law.

The course of legislation concerning realty has therefore been the opposite of that concerning personalty. In the former there has been simplification and the removal of superfluities; in the latter, elaboration and extension to meet new needs. A guiding impulse of legislation which has in recent years begun to bear some fruit, and may be expected to bear more in the future, has aimed at the gradual assimilation of the laws of realty and personalty, the model being, wherever possible, the law of personalty. The many inconveniences of having two systems of property-law sufficiently account for the impulse. With regard, however, to the rights of the owner of land, the principle of assimilation has been met by a counter-principle. Many hold with Mill that, since the raw material of the earth is not a product of labour, " property in land should be interpreted strictly, and the balance in all cases of doubt should incline against the proprietor[1]." Those who share this view would introduce a new distinction between real and personal property by reducing the rights of a landowner to a point below those of the owner of personalty.

A few words will serve to introduce our first two chapters concerning the very intricate and somewhat dry subject of the title and transfer of land. Ownership is analysed by general jurisprudence into rights of exclusive use and rights of alienation. The rights of alienation conferred by English law on the owner of land have during the last two centuries certainly been large enough and wide enough, so far as *legal* capacity has been concerned; indeed there is at the present day a strong tendency to consider them as having been too wide and too large. So defective, on the other hand, was the practical machinery of alienation both *inter vivos* and by will at the commencement of the Queen's

---

[1] *Political Economy*, Book ii. ch. ii. § 5.

reign, that not only was alienation a most vexatious and expensive proceeding, only to be undertaken under the pressure of strong motives, but the position of the alienee was in the highest degree insecure and precarious. With the rights of exclusive use and enjoyment it was fortunately otherwise. In the ordinary English tenure of common socage the rights of exclusive use recognized by the law sixty years ago were substantially complete enough to yield the best results not only for the owner but also for the community at large. The opinion of the Real Property Commissioners is worth reproducing : " When once," they reported, " the object of transactions respecting land is accomplished, and the estates and interests in it which are recognized are actually created and secured, the law of England, except in a few unimportant particulars, appears to come almost as near to perfection as can be expected in any human institutions[1]." The same is not true of leasehold tenure, nor of copyhold tenure, nor of some other peculiar tenures, as they existed at the beginning of the Queen's reign ; some account will be given of them in the third chapter. The same is not true even of common socage tenure, when the rights of the limited owner in possession are pared down by act of party below a certain point; a brief history of settlements or "entails" will be given in our second chapter.

[1] *First Report*, p. 6.

CHAPTER I.

LAND TRANSFER AND TITLE.

WHEN the Real Property Commissioners began their labours, the English law concerning the transfer of land was overgrown with defects and abuses to an extent almost incredible. There were indeed few direct legal limitations on the freedom of disposition. English judges had generally favoured the free alienation and the free circulation of land; even the rules against perpetuity were designed by them to limit the evil effects of the indulgence which had been extended to landowners during the Civil War of the seventeenth century, the power, namely, of tying up their lands by settlements on unborn persons. But while the power of disposition was almost unbounded, and certainly larger than that recognised by most foreign systems of law, the machinery of land transfer, and the safe-guards of title were inadequate and inefficient in the extreme. By the mere lapse of time, by the fact that since the reign of Edward I. there had been no general revision of the law, and by the inharmonious operation of promiscuous rules of law, the result had been brought about that of the land of England a large proportion was in one of two predicaments; "either the want of security against the existence of latent deeds rendered actually unsafe a title which was yet marketable, or the want of means of procuring the formal requisites of title rendered unmarketable a title which was substantially safe[1]." The diminution in the value of land which set in during the first quarter of the century was ascribed both by the Real Property Commissioners and by the landowners themselves to the "general feeling of the insecurity of title, and to the apprehension of the delay and expense attending transactions relating to real property[2]."

The causes of the expense and delay of land transfer and of the insecurity of title were found by the commissioners to consist in the difficulty of investigating and producing abstracts of title; the rules relating to dower; searches in registries; the rules relating to probates of wills and letters of administration; the practice of assigning attendant terms; the length and complexity of deeds; the rules concerning judgments; the execution of powers of appointment; the loss of deeds and the absence of effective covenants to produce; the rules of law relating to real actions and the statutes of limitation. A buyer of land had to wait long and pay much before the transaction was completed. During the first half of the century abstracts of title were long and expensive. Purchasers could hardly ever afford to accept less than sixty years' title, in fact strict proof of title was usually required for

[1] *Second Report, Real Property Commissioners*, p. 17.
[2] *Ibid.* p. 20.

ninety or a hundred years. This lengthy period was rendered necessary by the operation of the statutes of limitation and of the real actions. The Acts of Parliament, which had at various times altered and added to the common law period of limitation of a year and a day, had had small regard for uniformity or consistency. In addition to establishing different periods of limitation for different kinds of property, Parliament had created for the same kind of property many different periods of limitation depending not upon the length of adverse enjoyment, but upon the form of remedy selected by the claimant, or upon the doing of certain irrelevant acts by the party in possession. After an adverse possession of sixty years, by which the highest Real Action was barred, a writ of entry might still in some cases be put in force; on the other hand, a wrongful possessor was permitted, by going through certain forms which were in reality known only to himself and his legal advisers (although a fiction of the law supposed them to be made public), to bar the rightful owner in the short space of six years from the time when the right accrued[1]. In practice, indeed, claims could seldom be set up after twenty years' adverse possession; yet the instances in which they were successfully so set up rendered all titles questionable to the extreme limit of the period allowed to the real actions.

Another cause of expense and delay in proving title and transferring land was the law of dower. The Real Property Commissioners found that dower existed

[1] *First Report, Real Prop. Comm.* p. 40.

beneficially in very few cases; it was of little value considered as a provision for widows, and was never calculated on as a provision by females who contracted marriage, or by their friends[1]. At the same time there was so much uncertainty in the modes by which dower might be prevented, that the actual or possible existence of the right was a frequent and serious impediment to the transfer of property. "The necessity of ascertaining in each case of transfer that it did not exist in the widows of any of the persons through whom the property had passed, or procuring the necessary acts to be done for preventing or barring it, where it did or might exist, were the causes of frequent and great delay and expense attending such transfers[2]."

An even greater element of expense and delay in the transfer of land was to be found in the vicious practice of keeping on foot attendant terms. The system had been invented by lawyers to guard against latent defects of title; but the remedy proved worse than the disease. The procedure was as follows: Long terms of years vested in trustees were left in existence after their objects were satisfied, and became attendant on the inheritance. On a sale of land in which such a satisfied long term subsisted, the term was assigned to a trustee nominated by the purchaser, "on trust to attend the inheritance." The advantage of the proceeding lay in the protection which the purchaser obtained against possible incumbrances on the freehold, created after the commencement of the term and of which he had no notice at the time of the sale. But

[1] *First Report, Real Prop. Comm.* pp. 16 et seqq.
[2] *Ibid.* pp. 16 et seqq.

this advantage was purchased at an enormous cost.
In addition to the abstract of title to the freehold, an
abstract of title had often to be produced to each
attendant term assigned, and in consequence of the
numerous instances in which different attendant terms
comprised different portions of an estate, the number
of attendant terms to be assigned was often very
large[1]; in such cases it was generally advisable to
assign all the terms, in order to guard against the
difficulties which frequently arose in establishing a
term at law. It was also as a rule advisable to assign
a term in a separate deed which was frequently much
longer than the conveyance of the freehold[2]. Much
expense and difficulty, again, arose in finding the
trustees in whom the terms had been vested, or in
tracing their personal representatives, especially in the
complicated and defective state of the law with regard
to the granting of probate and letters of administration.
Even after the purchaser had with infinite trouble
obtained the assignment of all the attendant terms
of which he knew, the protection which they afforded
against incumbrances was precarious and often inadequate; their protection might easily be lost by
carelessness or by accident, by the operation of the
rules of law as to merger, or of the rules of equity as
to constructive notice and presumed surrender of
the term[3], or by the emergence of a term older than
those held by the purchaser. The conveyancing device
of attendant terms was, in short, a failure; it had
doubled, if not trebled, the cost and the delay of

---

[1] *Second Report, Real Prop. Comm.* p. 10.
[2] *Ibid.* pp. 8, 9.   [3] *Ibid.* p. 11.

land transfer without adding appreciably or proportionately to the security of purchasers.

Another cause which added to the expense of land transfer and the insecurity of title was one which may be considered inherent in all systems of conveyance by private and secret documents. Deeds are in their nature liable to get lost or mislaid, suppressed, substituted, or forged. The fact that a vendor possesses the title-deeds can never be a conclusive assurance to the purchaser. A tenant in fee-simple may make a settlement retaining for himself a life-estate only, and yet the deeds granting him a fee-simple estate may remain in his possession. So also a mortgager may regain possession of deeds from a mortgagee on some pretext or other. That the facilities for fraud are great under a system of private conveyances, appears abundantly from the evidence taken by the Real Property Commissioners[1]. It appears from the same evidence that estates (and especially the estates of mortgagees) were frequently defeated in consequence of latent defects of title arising from the fraudulent or negligent suppression of documents, and that even when no actual loss resulted to purchasers or mortgagees from such suppression, the danger had always to be guarded against by instituting expensive and dilatory inquiries into various collateral sources of information. A would-be purchaser of land had either to buy from a personal acquaintance of whose honesty he or his solicitor was assured, or he had to engage a private detective to examine the antecedent career and

---

[1] *Second Report*, p. 6, and references to evidence there given.

domestic history of the vendor[1]. The system of conveyance by private documents had the further result, equally unfortunate, that persons interested under deeds often had neither the possession nor the means of enforcing the production of those deeds. When, for example, an estate is divided, the same deed constitutes the title of several owners, the party retaining the deed usually covenanting to produce it when required. Covenants for the production of deeds were found by the Real Property Commissioners to be rarely effectual after alienation by either party to the covenant ; and even when the covenants were effectual, it was found that deeds were often lost " through being left with solicitors or remaining in the houses of life-tenants after their death[2]."

These circumstances rendered many titles unmarketable, and caused much difficulty and litigation to attend the transfer of real property. Some vendors attempted to avoid all difficulties by special conditions of sale precluding the purchaser from objecting to the title on account of the loss or non-production of deeds ; but such stipulations in the hands of rogues afforded the means of entrapping ignorant and unwary purchasers. It consequently became quite a frequent occurrence for both buyers and sellers of land to decline entering into any binding contract until the title had been approved ; then if both parties continued in the same mind, the purchase was made[3].

Other causes which in effect very often made land unsaleable, and which added to the expense and risk of

---

[1] *Second Report, Real Prop. Comm.* p. 7.
[2] *Ibid.* p. 16.   [3] *Ibid.* p. 17.

every transfer, were to be found in dormant judgments
and in the rules of construction of wills. Judgments
docketed in any court of law became liens on the estates
of the persons against whom they were entered up, and
on the estates which they might afterwards acquire.
On every purchase it was therefore necessary to search
for judgments in all the courts against every person
who might have been owner of any part of the estate.
The dockets or books contained the names without any
other description; and when a judgment was discovered
against the name of an owner, the person bound to show
a good title had to procure satisfactory proof that it
applied to another person of the same name. When
an estate had belonged to several persons, the expenses
of searching for judgments became enormous; and a
serious difficulty arose where the name of any of the
owners was one of common occurrence. Upwards of
500 judgments were to be found against such names as
Smith and Brown[1]; in such a case, it could hardly be
expected that the vendor should obtain certificates
from all the solicitors who obtained the judgments,
and yet there was no other means by which it could
be proved that the title was not affected by them.

Such were the preliminary difficulties which the
purchaser of land had to meet in order to assure
himself that the vendor possessed the estate which
he professed to sell. Turning now to the actual
conveyance, we find lengthiness, cumbrousness and expensiveness on every hand. These attributes of deeds
and legal documents were to a large extent rendered

[1] John Tyrrell's *Evidence*, p. 182.

inevitable by the wide powers of making complicated dispositions recognised by the law of England. A further proportion of their length was due to the fact that deeds had to perform a quasi-legislative function, by rendering inoperative inconvenient rules of law which had long existed only to be evaded. Of this nature were the uses to bar dower, the uses to preserve contingent remainders against destruction by forfeiture, surrender or merger, and the lease for a year which formed part of the ordinary form of conveyance. Needless to say, brevity and simplicity were impossible in documents filled with such "cumbrous contrivances to effect useful objects which the law afforded no direct or simple means of accomplishing." A third cause of the lengthiness of legal documents served no useful object but that of providing an adequate remuneration for lawyers. The vicious system of paying solicitors at a fixed price per folio was largely responsible for the fact that at the time of the Real Property Commission an ordinary purchase deed contained at least forty-two folios of writing, while each attendant term assigned required a deed of still greater length; the usual length of a marriage settlement was 110 folios[1].

After all the necessary documents had been duly drawn up and executed; after the evidence which could be obtained had been investigated with the greatest care, and every possible means of finding objections to it had been resorted to, there still remained some possible causes of insecurity which no vigilance or ingenuity could discover. Chief among these causes

---

[1] James Humphreys, *Real Property*, pp. 327 et seqq.

were the want of protection against the fraudulent suppression of settlements, mortgages and charges, the length of time after which dormant rights could be enforced, the existence of remainders and reversions after estates tail, the want of limitation of the remedies of the Crown and the Church in many cases, and the harassing and uncertain questions of law which might at any time emerge, particularly upon the construction of wills. Their aggregate effect is thus summed up by John Tyrrell : "No title can be considered at present to be perfectly safe[1]."

Matters affecting the title and transfer of land were much improved by the large amendments of law carried through at the recommendation of the Real Property Commissioners. The Dower Act of 1833[2] not only simplified the proof of title, but also enabled the "uses to bar dower" to be dispensed with; such uses were still inserted for some time in order to render proof of the date of marriage unnecessary, but conveyances were afterwards shortened by their universal omission. By the Real Property Limitation Act of 1833[3], again, the periods for the limitation of actions were shortened and rendered uniform; they were "so fixed as to give ample opportunity to assert just rights, and yet not to countenance claims which had long been dormant[4]." By the same Act the real actions, of whose mischiefs the Real Property Commissioners had given a most graphic account[5], were abolished, with the

---

[1] *Evidence*, p. 168 (1830 A.D.).
[2] 3 & 4 Will. IV. c. 105.   [3] *Ibid.* c. 27.
[4] *First Report, Real Prop. Comm.* pp. 39 et seqq.
[5] *Ibid.* pp. 42 et seqq.

exception of Dower and Quare Impedit[1]. Besides
adding greatly to the security of title, this Act rendered it possible by the middle of the century for
conveyancers to shorten the period of proof of title
from ninety to forty years on a purchase of land[2].
Both title and transfer were further simplified by the
Inheritance Act of 1833[3], which abolished the inconvenient rule of *seisina facit stipitem* with all its
capricious niceties, and by the Fines and Recoveries
Act[4] of the same year, which effected a great saving of
expense and trouble in the transfer of entailed lands.

The great and sovereign remedy, however, to which
the Real Property Commissioners pinned their faith,
was the compulsory registration of all assurances of real
property. By a General Register they hoped to cure
all evils; to render titles secure, fraud impossible, and
loss of deeds harmless; to abate the nuisance of
assigning satisfied terms; to remove the injustice done
to mortgagees by the tacking of securities, and the
defects of covenants to produce documents; and to
make it impossible for persons to be kept out of their
estates through ignorance of their own rights[5].

Seventy years of experience, and the opportunity
of observing the operation of foreign registries, have
made it possible to appreciate *a posteriori* the merits
and demerits of the Commissioners' scheme. Systems
of general registration are of two main kinds, differing
both in their object and in their mode of operation, viz.,

---

[1] 3 & 4 Will. IV. c. 27, s. 36.

[2] Joshua Williams, *The Transfer of Land* (1862), pp. 5 et seqq.

[3] 3 & 4 Will. IV. c. 106.   [4] *Ibid.* c. 74.

[5] *Second Report*, pp. 4–17.

the registration of Assurances and the registration of Title.

The chief object of registering assurances is to prevent fraud by securing publicity to every transaction. The principal object of registering titles is to facilitate and cheapen the transfer of land. The registration of title presents an intending purchaser or mortgagee with the *net* result of former dealings with the property, while the registration of assurances places the dealings themselves before him, and leaves him to investigate them for himself. In the one case he finds, so to speak, the sum worked out for him; in the other he has the figures given him and has to work out the sum for himself. The legal effect of a registration of assurances is merely to prove that a given document was filed in a given place at a given time; the legal effect of a registration of title is to prove that a given title was vested in a given person at a given time. Hence under a registration of assurances, the registered documents would still have to be examined on every successive conveyance; under a registration of title, there would be no necessity for investigations or for abstracts of title[1].

The subject of a general register had occupied the minds of Englishmen since the seventeenth century. While Sir Francis Bacon was Lord Keeper, letters patent had issued for the establishment of an " Office of General Remembrance of Matters of Record," but

---

[1] Report of Mr Osborne Morgan's Committee, *Parl. Pap.* 1879, vol. XI. pp. ix. et seqq., and evidence of Joshua Williams, questions 423–4, 458–60, and of Learoyd, qq. 1592, 1599, and of Lord Chancellor Cairns, q. 1881.

the scheme had fallen to the ground. During the Commonwealth the matter had engaged the attention of Parliament. In the reign of Charles II. a select committee of the House of Lords had declared its opinion that "one cause of the decay of rents and value of lands was the uncertainty of titles of estates"; and as a principal remedy they had proposed a "Bill of Registers." Since that time attempts had frequently been made to establish a general register. In despair of obtaining one, Middlesex and York established local registers and other counties applied for them. In 1740 a bill for a general register was nearly successful, but a serious opposition was offered by the clerks of the inrolment, whose fees would be affected by it; and the prospects of general registration subsequently declined[1]. The matter was not however lost sight of by the public. In 1789 Sir Francis Plowden published some "Impartial thoughts on the beneficial consequences of inrolling all deeds." In 1815 and 1816 bills were brought in for the "public registering" of assurances by Sergeant Onslow, supported by Sir Samuel Romilly; these bills came to grief owing to the petitions of certain maritime towns[2].

The demand for registration continued to be strongly voiced by Sugden, by Miller, Humphreys and Tyrrell. When the Real Property Commissioners met, suggestions and schemes flowed in from all sides. Much evidence was taken concerning the operation of foreign registries; and Jeremy Bentham wrote a long communication in

[1] Report of Registration Commission, *Parl. Pap.* 1850, vol. xxxii. pp. 3 et seqq.; and *ibid.* W. G. Sanders in Appendix, p. 274.

[2] *Comm. Journ.* lxxi. 308, 328.

his worst style, urging, in support of compulsory registration, two of the twenty-seven principles which he considered necessary for a thorough revision of the whole field of Real Property Law, viz.: (1) the "greatest-happiness principle, or the happiness-maximizing principle"; and (2) the "disappointment-minimizing" or "non-disappointment principle[1]." One of the witnesses, T. G. Fonnereau, suggested a registration of title as distinguished from a registration of assurances[2]. Of this suggestion no notice was taken.

The Commissioners proposed to establish a general metropolitan register (with sub-registers in several districts) for the registration at length of every document relating to real property by which any estate or charge was created or transferred at law or in equity (except such documents as related to copyholds or leases under twenty-one years). Both legal and equitable estates were to have priority according to the time of registration; the documents were to be classified under separate heads, and when a grantor in a document to be registered did not derive title through a registered document, the former document was to be at the head of a class, and would form a "root of title." There was further to be an alphabetical index to the documents standing at the head of the several classes and forming the roots of the several registered titles[3]. The Commissioners cheerfully dismissed all the objections which were advanced against

---

[1] *Second Report*, Appendix, pp. 440 et seqq.; and *Third Report*, Appendix, pp. 36 et seqq.

[2] *Second Report*, Appendix, pp. 11, 96.

[3] *Second Report*, pp. 28–47.

their scheme. It had been objected that the expense of the register would be too great; that the investigation of title on the register would not only be attended with uncertainty, but that both registration and investigation would cause delay in the transfer of land; that the register would disclose defects of titles, and would increase instead of diminishing their insecurity by making it possible to defeat a title by the prior registration of a document subsequently executed; that the safety of titles would therefore depend on the fidelity, skill and activity of solicitors; and lastly that the register would expose private transactions such as mortgages and family settlements.

A bill embodying the elaborate scheme of the Commissioners was introduced in 1830 by their President, John (afterwards Lord) Campbell; but before its second reading Parliament was dissolved. When the new Parliament met, John Campbell again introduced the bill, but before its second reading Parliament was prorogued owing to the rejection of the Reform Bill by the House of Lords[1]. In December 1831 the bill was again brought in and referred to a select committee, which after examining many witnesses reported unanimously in its favour, while advocating a reduction of charges in the interest of small purchasers. The country solicitors now took it into their heads that the bill would bring all conveyancing business to London. Petitions poured in from all parts of the kingdom, and it was alleged that registration was a deep scheme for enabling the Government to impose a new land-tax;

[1] Hansard, cxv. p. 6.

the public at large was so infuriated that the bill had to be dropped[1]. In 1833 and 1834 further attempts made by other members of Parliament to introduce registration schemes were defeated by large and increasing majorities, and the whole matter was abandoned in despair.

During the two succeeding years nothing was done to cheapen or simplify the title or the transfer of land. In 1837, however, the Wills Act introduced many incidental benefits[2]. An Act of 1841[3] abolished the lease for a year, thus diminishing the number of deeds in a conveyance by one; and by an Act of 1844[4] and the valuable Real Property Act of 1845[5] all fiction of a lease was abandoned, and corporeal hereditaments were declared to lie in grant. Another section of the Real Property Act[6] abolished the logical but inconvenient rule of the common law by which contingent remainders were liable to destruction through forfeiture, surrender or merger; this enactment has considerably shortened settlements by rendering unnecessary the insertion of trusts to preserve contingent remainders. As such remainders occur in almost all settlements, and as most of the land in England was then and is now in strict settlement, it will be realised what a saving of trouble and expense the Act has effected.

Other important improvements were introduced by the same Act. Feoffments, although they were no

---

[1] *Comm. Journ.* LXXXVIII. 342. [2] *Vide infra*, chap. IV.
[3] 4 & 5 Vict. c. 21. [4] 7 & 8 Vict. c. 76, s. 2.
[5] 8 & 9 Vict. c. 106, s. 2.
[6] 8 & 9 Vict. c. 106, s. 8, repealing 7 & 8 Vict. c. 76, to the same effect.

longer attended with any real publicity, still retained their feudal effect of creating estates by wrong, of working forfeitures, and of rendering the interest of the right owner incapable of disposition by deed or will. The Act conferred a great benefit on all land-owners by altogether abolishing the tortious operation of feoffments[1]. The same Act greatly improved the *status* of contingent remainders. Contingent remainders were devisable by will and assignable in equity, but not transferable at common law otherwise than by a fine, although they might be released. The reasons for this exceptional treatment were sufficiently technical; it was said that a contingent remainder was a mere possibility and the owner of it not in the seisin; or it was said, in the alternative, that a grant at common law, which was the proper mode of conveying remainders, required attornment to perfect its operation, and attornment was altogether inapplicable to the nature of a contingent remainder. In accordance with the recommendations of the Real Property Commissioners, the Act of 1845[2] made both contingent remainders and executory interests transferable at law by deed[3].

In the same year, 1845, Lord Brougham carried an Act[4], based on the recommendations of the Real Property Commissioners, "for abridging deeds by making certain powers and obligations legal incidents to certain estates and interests to which they are now almost uniformly annexed, or by recommending prescribed forms of conveyance to which in certain cases a given effect shall

---

[1] 8 & 9 Vict. c. 106, s. 4.   [2] *Ibid.* c. 106, s. 6.
[3] *Third Report*, pp. 346 et seqq.   [4] 8 & 9 Vict. c. 119.

be imputed[1]." The Act tried to render superfluous the insertion of "general words" at the end of the "parcels" of a deed, and of the "estate clause" which had originated in the old form of conveyance by lease and release; short forms of covenants for title and of the operative parts of conveyances were also provided. The Act, which is the forerunner of our modern Conveyancing Acts, was entirely neglected in practice[2], as might have been expected so long as conveyancers were paid by verbiage and not by results. In the same year the efforts of Lord Brougham effected a most substantial improvement in conveyancing by means of the Act "to render the assignment of satisfied terms unnecessary[3]." This Act, while preserving the protective power of existing satisfied terms, provided that for the future all satisfied terms should absolutely cease as soon as they should become attendant upon the inheritance or reversion of any land. It has been estimated by an eminent modern conveyancer that this enactment reduced the expense of land transfer by more than one-half[4].

Notwithstanding these important improvements, the tediousness and costliness of conveyances and mortgages continued to be keenly felt by the landowning classes, and a strong demand arose for some more radical change. Delay and expense, and uncertainty as to the delay and expense were the grievances complained of.

[1] *First Report of Real Prop. Comm.* p. 57.

[2] *Parl. Pap.* 1879, vol. XI. p. vii (Mr O. Morgan's Comm. Report).

[3] 8 & 9 Vict. c. 112.

[4] Lawrence (President Incorporated Law Society), *Presidential Address*, 1879, p. 8.

" It was," said Joshua Williams, " no slight cause of the
demand for change, that it was impossible for the
purchaser to know beforehand how great the delay or
the expense might be. That which disgusted the
purchaser of land was that when he went to an auction
or signed a contract no man could tell him how long he
might have to wait, or how much he might have to
pay, by the time the purchase was completed[1]." Conveyances being private and secret documents, frauds
and suppressions had still to be ever guarded against,
however rarely they might actually take place; the
necessity continued for elaborate searches, investigations
and inquiries " manifold, intricate, chargeable, tedious
and uncertain[2]." Constant difficulties continued to be
experienced, too, in obtaining the production of deeds
relating in common to two or more estates or to the
divided parts of an estate once entire; and the same
difficulties continued to render titles unmarketable and
caused endless disputes as to the proper custody of
title-deeds[3]. The rule of law, again, giving the possession
of title-deeds to the immediate freeholder still rendered
it impossible for a reversioner or remainderman to sell
his interest at an adequate price; and the want of a
central repertory for the deposit of deeds resulted in
continual losses of deeds and consequently in special
conditions of sale often so disguised as to entrap the
unlearned or unwary buyer[4]. But the most grievous

[1] Joshua Williams, *Transfer of Land*, 1862, p. 5.

[2] Report of Registration Commission, *Parl. Pap.* 1850, vol. xxxii.
p. 7.

[3] *Parl. Pap.* 1850, vol. xxxii. p. 8; and *ibid.* 1857, vol. xviii.
pp. 258, 259.

[4] *Ibid.* 1857, vol. xviii. pp. 259, 260.

feature of all these difficulties was their recurrence on
each successive sale or mortgage of the same estate or
plot of land. A history of prior dealings with the land
had to be investigated, recited, and embodied in an
abstract of title, on each succeeding disposition. As
Sir Hugh (afterwards Lord) Cairns put it: "Suppose
I buy an estate to-day. I spend a year, or two or
three years, in ascertaining whether the title is a good
one. I am at last satisfied. I pay the expense—the
considerable expense—which is incurred in addition
to the price which I have paid for my estate, and
I obtain a conveyance of my estate. About a year
afterwards I desire to raise money upon a mortgage
of this estate. I find someone willing to lend me
money provided I have a good title to the estate.
The man says: 'It is very true that you bought this
estate and that you investigated the title, but I cannot
be bound by your investigation of the title, nor can
I be satisfied by it. My solicitor must examine the
title, and my counsel must advise on it.' And then
there is a repetition of the process which took place
upon my purchase of the estate, and consequently the
same expense is incurred as when I bought it; and
afterwards, if I want to sell the estate outright, the
same process is repeated and the same expense is
incurred again[1]."

Impressed with this condition of things, Lord
Campbell in 1845 and in 1846 introduced in the
House of Lords Registration bills similar to those of
1830 and 1831. In 1846 a Select Committee of the

---

[1] Hansard, 1859, vol. CLII. pp. 281 et seqq.

House, appointed to inquire into the burdens on real
property and the impediments to agricultural transactions, took volumes of evidence on the depreciation of
landed property, the unsatisfactory state of agriculture,
and the advantages which had resulted from the
registration of deeds in Scotland and Ireland; and
they were particularly impressed by what they heard
concerning the facility of dealings with landed property
in foreign countries[1]. In their report, while acknowledging the benefits of the Satisfied Terms Act, they
desired to impress on the House " the necessity of a
thorough revision of the whole subject of conveyancing,
and the disuse of the existing prolix, expensive and
vexatious system "; and they were of opinion that a
registry of deeds was essential to the success of any
attempt to simplify that system. They ascribed the
serious diminution in the value of real property to the
tedious and expensive process of the transfer of land,
and their first and foremost recommendation for
ameliorating the wretched state of English agriculture
was " the improvement of the *forms of conveyance,* and
the establishment of some effective system for the
registration of deeds[2]."

In consequence of this Report, a Royal Commission
was in 1847 appointed to consider whether the burdens
on land could be diminished by an effective system for
the registration of deeds and the simplification of the
forms of conveyance. The Commissioners heard much
evidence and received much information about foreign
registries, and reported three years later that " the

---

[1] *Parl. Pap.* 1846, vol. vi. parts i. and ii.
[2] *Ibid.* 1846, vol. vi. pt. i. pp. xii., xiii.

positive expenses attaching themselves to land whenever an assurance of it was effected arose from the
artificial and intricate mode of conveyancing consequent
upon the state of the law; that the *delay* of land
transfer was a burden even more serious than the
expense; and that the *fear* of the delay, as well as of
the expense, was a more effective cause of the depreciation of land than the apprehension that a title might
be insecure after the completion of a sale or mortgage.
The experience of the delay, especially, which so often
attended sales and transfers, by deterring some persons
from making investments in land, and others from
lending on mortgage, materially diminished the value
of landed property[1]."

The Commissioners proceeded to recommend a
system of registration of assurances very similar to
that of the Real Property Commissioners of 1830, but
carried out to an even greater degree of elaboration.
Its immediate object was stated to be to secure purchasers of land against fraud; to enable a purchaser
to assure himself readily that no document was in
existence which could defeat or alter the title offered
to him, and to afford him, when he accepted a conveyance, prompt and easy means of securing his own
title[2].

In the following year (1851) Lord Campbell introduced a bill founded on these recommendations.
It was strongly opposed by the Incorporated Law
Society, on the grounds that it would diminish instead
of increasing the number of transfers of land; that it

---

[1] *Parl. Pap.* 1850, vol. xxxii. pp. 7, 8.
[2] *Ibid.* 1850, vol. xxxii. p. 8.

would act adversely to the sale and purchase of *small*
properties in land, and would lead to a dangerous
disclosure of family arrangements and settlements[1].
The bill passed through the House of Lords, but came
to grief in the Commons. A similar bill was brought
in two years later by Lord Cranworth, then Lord
Chancellor. It passed through the Lords; in the
Commons it was read twice and referred to a Select
Committee[2]. The evidence given before the Committee,
and especially the evidence of Mr W. S. Cookson[3], re-
volutionised all its preconceived ideas on the subject
of registration. The Committee reported that they
had discovered two distinct principles of registration,
one contemplating the registration of *assurances*, the
other contemplating a registration of the *legal title*
to land. " Pursuing this idea, and confining their
attention to this distinction," the Committee had
noticed "a scheme for the registration of title or of
legal ownership, which if fully developed would fulfil
the most important conditions of registration." They
therefore recommended that Lord Cranworth's Registration bill should be dropped and a Royal Commission
appointed to consider the subject of the registration
of title[4].

A Commission was appointed early in the following
year. After examining many solicitors and conveyancers, and receiving some valuable suggestions from
Joshua Williams[5], the Commissioners reported, in 1857,

[1] Hansard, cxv. p. 562.
[2] *Ibid.* cxxvi. 1230.   [3] *Parl. Pap.* 1853, vol. xxxvi. qq. 1–221.
[4] *Parl. Pap.* 1853, vol. xxxvi. pp. 397 et seqq.
[5] *Ibid.* 1857, vol. xviii. Appendix, pp. 306 et seqq.

to the effect that there existed a general insecurity of title and apprehension of risk; and that the investigation of titles caused not only expense, but "delay, annoyance and disappointment, sickening both to buyer and seller. The seller does not receive his money, nor the buyer his land, until the advantage or the pleasure of the bargain is lost or has passed away."

The recommendations of the Commission were numerous and important. They decided on a Registry of Title as distinguished from a Registry of Assurances, and they advocated many other miscellaneous improvements in the law of Real Property.

With regard to the Registry of Title, their proposals have been thus summarised[1]: The leading principle was that the fee-simple title alone should be registered subject to the exception that charges and leases should have a separate registry of their own. In accordance with this principle, beneficial interests less than the fee-simple, and dealings with such interests, were not to be registered or at least not registered in the register of the fee, for such a system would practically amount to a registry of assurances. The registered title was not to amount necessarily to a "parliamentary" or unimpeachable title. Equitable interests were to be protected by cautions or notices on the register. It was to be competent to a landowner to register with a statutory or indefeasible title if he desired it, and such a title was to be guaranteed by the State.

[1] By the Registration Commission of 1870, *Parl. Pap.* 1870, vol. xviii. p. x.

In 1858 Lord Cranworth unsuccessfully attempted to carry this scheme through Parliament. In 1859 two Registration bills were introduced by Sir Hugh Cairns, then Solicitor-General, but it was not till 1862 that an Act for the Registration of Titles was carried by Lord Westbury. Of this Act[1], commonly known as "Lord Westbury's Act," the main features were:

(1) Registration of Title under the Act was not compulsory; it was purely optional, and even a registered title could be withdrawn from the register at pleasure.

(2) Application for registration could be made only by the person having or having the power to dispose of the whole fee, or by the several persons having collectively this title or capacity.

(3) All derivative estates, interests and powers were placed on the register.

(4) The title to be shown on an application to register a title as indefeasible, was required to be a "valid marketable title," *i.e.* such as would be forced by the Courts of Equity on an unwilling purchaser.

(5) All titles registered under the Act were made indefeasible, either immediately or at a future time, for the purpose of sales, mortgages and contracts for valuable consideration.

(6) The title registered was to be subject to registered charges and incumbrances; unregistered interests also could be protected by the entry of *caveats* on the register.

(7) There was a separate register for certain leasehold interests.

---

[1] 25 & 26 Vict. c. 53.

It is easy to see that the Act departed widely from
the recommendations of the Royal Commission of
1854–7, especially in not confining the registration
to the fee-simple alone, and in making no provision
for the registration of defeasible, qualified or merely
possessory titles. The subsequent history of the Act
will be later dealt with.

In the same year, 1862, Lord Westbury carried
another Act[1] " for obtaining a Declaration of Title."
By this Act persons claiming to be entitled to land in
fee-simple, or claiming power to dispose of land in fee-
simple, were empowered to apply to the Court of
Chancery for a declaration of title; the title was to be
investigated by the Court, and if the Court were satisfied
that the title was such as it would compel an unwilling
purchaser to accept, an order was to be made (subject
to appeal) establishing the title, and a certificate of
title issued. The Act has been a dead letter from its
commencement, no application under it having ever
been made to the Court of Chancery[2].

Of the miscellaneous improvements recommended
by the Royal Commission of 1854–7, some were
carried out by Lord St Leonards in the Law of
Property Amendment Act, 1859[3], commonly called
" Lord St Leonards' Act." As the law then stood,
leasehold and personal property, not coming within
the Statute of Uses, could only be conveyed by a person
to himself jointly with another by means of two
separate conveyances. Lord St Leonards' Act has

[1] 25 & 26 Vict. c. 67.

[2] *Report of Bar Committee*, 25 March 1886, p. 32.

[3] 22 & 23 Vict. c. 35.

made a single and direct assignment sufficient[1]. This improvement (originally suggested by Joshua Williams) has been of immense service in facilitating and simplifying marriage settlements[2]. Another section of Lord St Leonards' Act greatly improved the law relating to the execution of powers of appointment otherwise than by will. Before the Act a power of appointment could be validly exercised, where no form was prescribed in the deed, by a mere writing. In order to avoid this laxity of the law, donors of powers usually prescribed forms of execution with more or less minuteness. The variety of different ceremonies occurring in practice gave rise to many vexatious questions whether they had been properly complied with, the Courts of Law requiring a strict compliance, while the Courts of Equity were perhaps over-generous in affording relief. Lord St Leonards' Act, adopting the proposals of the Real Property Commission and of the Royal Commission of 1854–7[3], while allowing donees of a power to execute it conformably to the power, and while saving certain formalities tending to prevent fraud and undue influence, provided that a deed attested by two witnesses should be a valid and sufficient execution of any power of appointment other than a power of appointment by will.

In the following year, 1860, Lord Cranworth made an attempt, similar to that made by Lord Brougham in 1845, to shorten deeds by rendering powers of sale, etc.,

[1] 22 & 23 Vict. c. 35, s. 21.

[2] Joshua Williams, *Transfer of Land*, p. 43.

[3] *First Report, Real Prop. Comm.* p. 58, and *Parl. Pap.* 1857, vol. xviii., Appendix, part B, pp. 394 et seqq.

incident to every mortgage or charge made by deed, unless a contrary intention were expressed by the parties. " Lord Cranworth's Act[1]," so far as it was meant to shorten deeds, has been a dead letter or nearly so[2]; indeed all such legislation was idle so long as the system of remunerating solicitors "put a premium upon verbiage." Certain other provisions of the Act have been more successful; the implied powers for the appointment of new trustees, in particular, have frequently been relied on in practice[3].

---

[1] 23 & 24 Vict. c. 145.

[2] *Parl. Pap.* 1879, vol. xi. p. vi (Report of Mr O. Morgan's Committee).

[3] Williams' *Conveyancing Statutes*, pp. 137 et seqq.

CHAPTER II.

LAND TRANSFER AND TITLE (*continued*).

THE improvements in land transfer described in
the preceding chapter were mainly due to the pressure
of the burden of expense and delay on the landowners
themselves. They had to bear this burden whenever
they found it necessary to deal with their land either
by way of sale, mortgage, or settlement. In all cases
the expense of making out the title fell on the owner;
the purchaser indeed paid for the verification of the
title and the preparation of the assurances, but upon a
mortgage or a settlement all charges whatsoever were
borne by the owner[1]. Not only the Tories and Con-
servatives, but also the later Whigs and the older
Liberals, were landowners, and the efforts of a landowning Parliament were naturally directed towards
diminishing the tax payable to conveyancers. Perhaps,
also, Parliament realised the elementary economic
principle, proclaimed by Mill[2], that "whatever facilitates the sale of land (as of any other sort of property)

---

[1] Sugden, *V. and P.* 406, 429.

[2] *Political Economy*, Bk. v. ch. IX. § 3.

tends to make it a more productive instrument for the
community at large; whatever prevents and restricts
its sale subtracts from its usefulness." Whether this
proposition was admitted or not, we at all events find
no practical proof of any deep policy for promoting the
welfare of the community at large by facilitating the
dispersion and division of the land. On the contrary,
it was the avowed policy of statesmen up to the time
when " Lord Westbury's Act " became law, to prevent
all legislative inroads on the existing distribution of
the land of England. For more than a century this
policy had pervaded the statute-book; so recently
indeed as 1856 Lord Palmerston could still inform his
Attorney-General that he " considered it essential to
the proper working of our constitution to preserve as
far as possible the practice of hereditary succession to
unbroken masses of landed property[1]." According to
Mr Charles Fyffe, the historian of Modern Europe, this
policy was due to the notions prevalent in England
about the time of the French Revolution. It was
thought that the safety of the State depended on the
class of landowners; " that they were the pillar of the
State, and that if the central pillar were removed, the
community would be exposed to the same collapse as
was seen to be going on on the Continent[2]."

It will also have been noticed thus far that law-
reformers and royal commissions ascribed the expense

[1] In a letter to Sir Richard Bethell (afterwards Lord Westbury)
quoted by the Small Holdings Committee, *Parl. Pap.* 1890, vol. xvii.
p. 189 ; and *ibid.* 1889, C. A. Fyffe, *Evidence*, qq. 6009 et seqq.

[2] Report of Small Holdings Committee, *Parl. Pap.* 1889, vol. xii.
questions 6013, 6024 et seqq.

of land transfer and the insecurity of title to more or
less superficial causes such as the absence of a repertory
for deeds, the bad system of paying solicitors, or small
anomalies in the law of real property. None of the
evil was ascribed to the practice of making complicated
settlements and of tying up the land; the Real Property
Commissioners, on the contrary, regarded that practice
with much complacency. "The owner of the soil," they
observed, "is invested with exactly the power and
dominion over it required for the public good, and
landed property in England is admirably made to
answer all the purposes to which it is applicable.
Settlements bestow on the present possessor of land
the benefits of ownership, and secure the property to
his posterity. In England families are preserved, and
purchasers always find a supply of land in the market[1]."

In the period with which we are now proceeding to
deal we shall find this judgment widely contradicted;
we shall find a conviction spreading among jurists and
statesmen that this same practice of making intricate
dispositions of land is the fundamental root of the
troubles besetting title and conveyance. A distinction has been recognised between the power of freely
alienating land, and the power of controlling the career
of that land after alienating it, and a disposition has
arisen to limit the latter while preserving and facilitating the exercise of the former power.

A sociological controversy which has had some
influence on recent property-legislation, and may be
expected to have still more influence in the future, has

---

[1] *First Report*, pp. 6, 7.

busied itself for many years about the best and fittest distribution of land amongst the members of a political community. Political economists have long recognised certain economic advantages attaching to small ownerships of land. Adam Smith, for example, wrote about large hereditary estates: "Compare their present condition with the possessions of the small proprietors in the neighbourhood, and you will require no other argument to convince you how unfavourable such extensive property is to improvement[1]." Cobden, again, in his famous Rochdale speech coined the phrase "free trade in land" and suggested the application of free trade principles to the agricultural economy of the country[2]. But neither the legislature nor the general public of England was much troubled with ideas about the proper distribution of land, until the results of the great proprietary reconstruction of the Continent by the French Revolution were sufficiently ascertained to render possible a comparison with the existing English system of landholding. About fifty years ago the subject was introduced to the English public by Joseph Kay, whose observations of men and manners had resulted in a comparison very disadvantageous to England. Kay's conclusions received the support of Mill, and have been emphasized and expanded by a legion of later political and economic writers, among whom may be mentioned Mr Thornton, Mr McDonnell, Mr Arthur Arnold, Mr Osborne Morgan, Mr Shaw Lefevre.

In the year 1869 and the following years Parliament

---

[1] *Wealth of Nations*, Bk. III. ch. II.   [2] *Speeches*, vol. II. p. 367.

received reports from Her Majesty's representatives concerning land-tenure in foreign countries. So far as these reports can be summarized and generalized, they were to the effect that in the States of central, northern and western Europe reforms had been carried through at the end of the last or the beginning of the present century with the object of promoting free traffic in land and preventing its accumulation in a few hands. These reforms had generally consisted in the abolition of entails, the establishment of systems of land transfer by registration or public notarial act, and, in many cases, the introduction of compulsory partition of inheritances together with the abolition of primogeniture. The reports concur in testifying that as a result of these reforms the land had become subdivided (but hardly ever excessively so) among small proprietors, cultivating each his own land; that this had caused a marked increase in agricultural production; that in those countries in which isolated large farms still existed, the *grande culture* compared unfavourably with the *petite culture*; that the small-farm system was everywhere found to stimulate industry and thrift to an incredible extent, and was attended with an almost complete absence of pauperism and with a general prosperity and well-being far beyond that of either the tenant-farmer or the agricultural labourer in England.

The rural condition and the distribution of land in England may best be gathered from the " New Domesday Book " of 1874[1] and from the Report and Evidence of the Small Holdings Committee of 1890[2].

---

[1] *Parl. Pap.* 1874, vol. LXXII.

[2] *Ibid.* 1890, vol. XVII. pp. 185 et seqq.

Of the area of England and Wales, one-half is owned
by 2250 persons, averaging 7300 acres each; 1750
other persons own between 1000 and 2000 acres
each, with an aggregate of 2,500,000 acres[1]; while
the yeomen farmers or peasant proprietors have practically ceased to exist[2]. The distinctive feature of the
English rural system is now " the complete separation
of the three classes—the landowners, the farm-tenants,
and the labourers[3]." The landowner supplies the land
and the capital required for all permanent improvements, such as draining and fencing, farmhouses and
labourers' cottages. The tenant has no permanent
interest in the land; he hires his farm generally on
a mere year-to-year tenancy. He hires the agricultural
labourers and supervises the work of the farm; he
expends nothing on permanent improvements, supplying only such capital as is necessary for the ordinary
cultivation of the land and for stocking it with sheep
and cattle. The agricultural labourers supply only
their labour. They have no interest whatever in the
land; they are engaged by the week or year; and
they have in many districts lost, by the enclosure of
commons, the rights which they formerly enjoyed[4].

The reasons for this state of things are not far to
seek. The same causes which formerly led to the
accumulation of land in a few hands on the continent
of Europe are still in operation in England. It has
been declared by the most distinguished economists,
statesmen and lawyers,—and it can hardly be denied—

[1] Shaw Lefevre, *Agrarian Tenures*, ch. i.

[2] *Parl. Pap.* 1890, vol. xvii. p. 187.

[3] Lefevre, *Agrar. Ten.* p. 4.   [4] *Ibid.* pp. 4 et seqq.

that the practice of tying up land by entails or family
settlements, the law of primogeniture, and the excessive
cost and delay of land transfer, have all operated to
prevent the natural dispersion of property in land.
It is indeed demonstrable that from the moment when
the English judges in the seventeenth century yielded
to landowners the right of tying up their estates by
settlements, the number of small freeholders began to
decrease and has continued to decrease[1]; and it has
been specifically found by the Small Holdings Committee of 1890 that the excessive legal expenses and
costs of land transfer are frequently prohibitive in the
case of small purchasers[2]. Another legislative cause
of the diminution of the number of small ownerships
is to be found in the past law and practice with regard
to the enclosure of commons[3]. While all these causes
have made for diminution in the number of small
freeholds, there has been no corresponding influence
to supply the leakage. Mr Fyffe has compared the
state of things to "a congested Railway Station in
which the down-line is blocked, while the up-line trains
are constantly coming into the Station; land is bought
up and put into settlement, and once there it stays
there, whereas under natural causes there would be
a flux both ways[4]." So again the Small Holdings
Committee have reported that "they could not doubt
that the distinct object of legislation down to a very
recent period was to prevent the dispersion of large
estates; and they believed that owing to this policy

[1] *Parl. Pap.* 1890, vol. XVII. p. 187.
[2] *Ibid.* p. 191.   [3] *Ibid.* p. 189.
[4] *Ibid.* 1889, vol. XII. Evidence, qq. 6056 et seqq.

the small ownerships which had been absorbed from time to time by large estates had remained attached to them, and had been thereafter and generally only purchaseable in large masses."

Not only have small freeholds practically disappeared, but within the last sixty years small tenancies too have almost vanished. This has been chiefly due to the practice of "consolidating farms" which prevailed so widely for a generation previous to the recent agricultural depression. The practice was formerly enjoined on landlords on economical grounds. It was asserted that the expense of keeping buildings in repair was much greater in proportion on small than on large farms, and that the employment of machinery and of the best agricultural methods was facilitated by the single management and cultivation of a large area; it was contended that small husbandry, like hand-loom weaving, was barbarous and antiquated, and that agriculture, like manufactures, should be conducted on a large scale and under the most scientific conditions[1].

The English rural system, then, is one of large estates and large tenancies worked by landless labourers. The social advantages of the system when seen at its best are considerable. The landlord is generous and benevolent, like Lord Lytton's Squire Hazeldean, and takes an intelligent guiding interest in the welfare both of tenants and labourers. These benefits however are precarious and are replaced by greater disadvantages not only in all cases where the landlord is non-resident, but also whenever estates are heavily

[1] *Parl. Pap.* 1890, vol. XVII. p. 188.

mortgaged or encumbered with family charges, or
cottages are overcrowded, unsanitary and in disrepair[1].

With regard to the relative economic advantage of
large and small properties, no definite conclusion has
yet been reached. It is maintained on the one hand
that small holdings are more productive in proportion
to their area than large ones, owing to the greater
energy displayed by those who with their families take
a personal part in the cultivation of the land; that
even when the small cultivator is only a tenant he is
profuse of his own labour, and can thus obtain results
which would be impossible to the large farmer compelled to pay at the market rate for every hour of work
on his farm. The agricultural returns appear to show
that small holdings carry a larger proportionate amount
of stock, other than sheep, than large ones, and that
the small cultivator pays, and is able to pay, a higher
proportionate rent than large cultivators. It is also
conceded generally that for all minor agricultural
produce such as fruit and vegetables, the small cultivator has the advantage[2]. On the other hand the
Central Chamber of Agriculture, and many persons
who can speak with authority, maintain that large
cultivation is necessarily more productive than small,
owing to the larger capital employed and the increased
use of machinery and scientific methods; and that this
is especially true " whenever the conformation of the
country allows of large evenly-shaped enclosures, and

[1] The social aspect of our rural system is sketched by Mr Shaw
Lefevre, *Agrar. Ten.* pp. 23 et seqq.

[2] *Vide* Report of Small Holdings Committee, *Parl. Pap.* 1890,
vol. XVII. pp. 186 et seqq.

where the soil and climate are adapted to the growth
of cereals and the rearing of sheep[1]."

There is no like divergence of opinion with regard
to the political and social advantages of small ownerships. Distinguished witnesses of all classes and of all
opinions examined by the Small Holdings Committee
of 1890 concurred in the view that an increase of
small cultivators would be a distinct "national and
social advantage." All agreed that the existence of a
numerous and prosperous peasantry was a condition of
national safety, and that the more general distribution
of land would lead to the security of property and to
the contentment of the population. All agreed, likewise, as to the effect upon character of the responsibility
involved in the secure possession of small holdings; all
testified to the "industry, thrift, and other civic
virtues" of small holders, whether owners or tenants.
They specially urged that the creation of small holdings
would check that migration of agricultural labourers
into the towns which has to some extent depopulated
the rural districts, and has at the same time intensified
the competition for employment in manufacturing
cities. The best among the agricultural labourers, in
despair of bettering their position, have flocked to the
towns; the rural population has thus deteriorated by
what Mr Fyffe calls "the survival of the unfittest[2]."
"Where facilities exist for the creation of small holdings," the Committee reports, "the ordinary labourer
has encouragement and hope; he sees an opportunity
for getting his foot on the first step of the ladder by

---

[1] *Ubi supra.*   [2] *Parl. Pap.* 1889, vol. XII. Evidence, q. 6202.

which he may win a better position. Without that hope he is only a bird of passage; there is no national sentiment in his heart. In the absence of a home a man has very little to look for[1]."

The principles of rural economy here described have in recent times been accepted more and more generally as guiding principles of legislation. In its earlier stages the agitation for the distribution of land was confined to the Liberal party; but the crisis which followed the beginning of the agricultural depression in 1879, combined with the alarming increase of redundant population in the towns, forced the subject on the attention of the legislature as a whole[2]. The question reached an acute stage after the agricultural labourers themselves had been admitted to the franchise in 1884. The distribution of land was placed prominently before the electorate; and when the new Parliament met in 1886, Mr Jesse Collings[3] moved as an amendment to the Address (which referred to the absence of improvement in the condition of the agricultural classes) that "The House humbly expressed its regret that no measures were announced for affording facilities to the agricultural labourers to obtain allotments and small holdings." In the course of the great debate which followed, Mr Gladstone expressed his admiration for small ownerships in land. "In face of the facts," he declared, "of French increase in wealth during the present century, the Right Honourable

---

[1] Report, *Parl. Pap.* 1890, vol. XVII. p. 185; *vide* also Mr Chaplin in 1892, Hansard, IVth series, vol. I. p. 911.

[2] Hansard, 1882, CCLXIX. 941; CCLXXIII. 1670.

[3] *Ibid.* CCCII. 443.

Gentleman (Mr Chaplin) ought to be slow in con-
demning that system[1]." On a division the amendment
was carried by a large majority and the government
resigned. Four years later the Small Holdings Committee, composed of men of all parties, reported
unanimously through their chairman, Mr Chamberlain,
that the extension of a system of small holdings was
a "matter of national importance." Still more recently
the desirability of the diffusion of land has been
acknowledged not only by legislative measures such
as the Small Agricultural Holdings Act of 1892, but
also by the most unequivocal declarations of leading
statesmen. In 1891 Lord Herschell declared in Parliament that it "had certainly been the policy of late
years to encourage the holding of land by as many
persons as possible[2]." In 1892, again, Mr Chaplin,
then President of the Board of Agriculture, stated on
behalf of the Government : " One of the chief objects
which we have in view is a wider distribution of the
land among the people ; to bring back to the soil, if it
be possible by legislation, a class of the community
now rapidly becoming extinct, namely yeomen or
owners of small properties in land[3]." So, again, Lord
Salisbury in 1892: " I am very anxious to multiply
small holdings. I do not think that small holdings
are the most economical way of cultivating the land.
But there are things more important than economy.
I believe that a small proprietary constitutes the
strongest bulwark against revolutionary change, and
affords the soundest support for the conservative

[1] Hansard, cccii. 465.   [2] *Ibid.* ccclv. 318.
[3] *Ibid.* ivth series, vol. i. p. 911.

feelings and institutions of this country[1]." Sir William
Harcourt, lastly, has vouched for the unanimity of the
Liberal party on the subject of attaching the labourer
to the soil[2].

It appears then that for one reason or another the
wider diffusion of ownership in land has during the
last fifty years tended to become, and has in recent
times actually become, a guiding principle of English
legislation. It may indeed be said to pervade our
recent legislation concerning real property. Its chief
practical results have consisted in the simplification
of title to real estate, in attempts to reduce the delay
and expense of land transfer, in actual or projected
interferences with the practice of tying up land by complicated dispositions, and in other legislative measures
to be later noticed. Possessed of this clue, we can
now resume the history of land transfer and title,
remembering that the dissatisfaction inspired by the
existing English rural system and the desire for the
wider distribution of land have intensified and given
a new significance to the demand for easier and cheaper
methods of conveyancing.

Lord Westbury's Registration Act of 1862 was
not a success. The total number of original titles
registered under the Act between 1863 and 1877 was
410 ; and the total number of titles, both original and
derivative, registered under the Act between 1863 and
1885 was 2673[3]. A Royal Commission was appointed
in 1868 to inquire into the operation of the Act.

[1] Exeter Speech, 3 Feb. 1892, quoted in Lefevre, *Agrar. Ten.*

[2] Hansard, 22 Feb. 1892.

[3] *Parl. Pap.* 1879, vol. XI. p. 183.

After taking much evidence, they reported in 1870 that the failure of the Act was due to three causes : the trouble, expense, and delay of registration, which far exceeded those of an ordinary sale; the fear of litigation in consequence of the notices which were required to be served on the various persons interested in the registered land; and the prospect of having to load the title, when once registered, with a record of every subsequent transaction. These causes the Commissioners thought to be inherent in the structure of the Act, and that chiefly because it required all titles to be without blemish, whereas purchasers were willing to overlook small blemishes; because it required all titles to be sixty years long, whereas purchasers were content with less, and mortgagees also; and because it required that the description of the land registered (boundaries and parcels) should bind strangers, whereas purchasers were content to make their own inquiries on such matters[1].

To avoid these difficulties for the future, the Commissioners proposed that a new Statute should be passed for the registration of title. They recommended that the register should be confined to the absolute fee-simple, particular estates and interests being protected by *caveats*; that a "good" though not technically a "valid marketable" title should be sufficient for registration; that short and even merely possessory titles should be capable of registration as such; that a "real representative" should be entered on the register in the place of a deceased registered owner, such

---

[1] *Parl. Pap.* 1870, vol. XVIII. pp. xix et seqq.

representative to have the same power to deal with the fee-simple as an executor or administrator has to deal with chattel interests; that registration should still be optional, but that a title once registered should not be removed from the register[1].

A bill founded on these recommendations was brought in by Lord Chancellor Selborne in 1873, making registration compulsory on the first change of ownership of any land thereafter. It was subsequently considered that the Judicature Act of the same year would interfere with the provisions of the bill, which was accordingly dropped. The bill was re-introduced in the following session by Lord Cairns with some modifications, but still retaining its compulsory character. Solicitors and conveyancers considered generally that the bill would impede small sales and mortgages, and laid such evidence before Lord Cairns that he felt constrained to except from his compulsory clauses all transactions under £300. The compulsory character of the bill nevertheless proved fatal to its progress. It was brought in again in the following year (1875) in a purely optional form, and became law[2].

Its main features follow the suggestions of the Land Transfer Commission of 1868–70. It restricted the registration to the beneficial fee-simple or to the power to convey the beneficial fee-simple[3]. Particular estates and partial interests (except leases for a life or twenty-one years unexpired, which were registered in a separate register) were protected by *caveats*. The Act permitted titles to be registered either as

[1] *Parl. Pap.* 1870, xviii. pp. xxvii et seqq.
[2] 38 & 39 Vict. c. 87.   [3] *Ibid.* s. 5.

(1) absolute, or (2) qualified, or (3) possessory, *i.e.*
subject to all estates, claims or interests existing at
the time of registration[1]. In order to register a title
as indefeasible, it was not required that an absolutely
flawless title should be shown ; if the Registrar were
of opinion that the title was indeed open to objection,
but was nevertheless a title, the holding under which
would not be disturbed, he might approve of it for
registration as absolute, *i.e.* indefeasible. The description, lastly, of property registered under the Act was
not conclusive as to the boundaries or the extent of
the property.

Before pursuing the history of this thoughtfully
devised Act, we have briefly to notice two Statutes
carried by Lord Cairns in 1874. Both have had a
most beneficial effect in shortening deeds and abstracts
of title and in generally diminishing the delay and
expense of conveyance[2]. The first was the Real
Property Limitation Act of 1874[3]. Acting upon a
suggestion of Lord St Leonards, this Act reduced from
twenty to twelve years the time for recovering land
or money charged upon land. The second was the
Vendor and Purchaser Act of 1874[4]. By this Statute
the period for the proof of title in open contracts for
the sale of land was reduced to forty years; in consequence of the legislative changes of 1833 it had become
unusual for purchasers to require the older sixty years'
title. The Act also gave legislative sanction (in the
absence of contrary stipulation) to the conveyancing

[1] 38 & 39 Vict. c. 87, ss. 8, 9, 18.
[2] *Vide Parl. Pap.* 1879, vol. xi. p. iii.   [3] 37 & 38 Vict. c. 57.
[4] 37 & 38 Vict. c. 78.

practice of making recitals and descriptions in deeds
twenty years old conclusive evidence unless proved
inaccurate.   It has further greatly facilitated transfers
of land by providing for the decision, upon summons in
chambers, of questions arising upon contracts for the
sale of land[1].

To return to the Land Transfer Act of 1875.
Notwithstanding the sedulous care with which it
avoided the errors of Lord Westbury's Act of 1862,
it proved an even more conspicuous failure.   In the
first three years of its existence only 48 titles were
registered under it; in the year 1878 only six[2].   The
obvious and sufficient reason of its failure was of course
its optional and permissive character.   But there was
an obstacle in the way of its success which would
probably have caused its breakdown even if it had
been compulsory.   We have said that registration
under the Act was confined to the fee-simple or to the
power of disposing of the fee-simple, and that lesser
estates were left to be protected by cautions, notices,
and inhibitions.   Unfortunately, however, more than
half the land of England and Wales is not held in fee-
simple and cannot be disposed of in fee-simple (apart
from powers of sale contained in settlements) by any
one person.   The greater portion of the land is leased
for long or short terms of years, settled on successive
holders by way of trust or otherwise, charged with

---

[1] Joshua Williams' *Transfer of Land*, pp. 5 sq. ; *Bar Committee's
Report*, 25 March 1886, pp. 6 sq.   Some other provisions of the
Vendor and Purchaser Act were afterwards incorporated in the
Conveyancing Act 1881.   *Vide infra*, p. 52.

[2] *Parl. Pap.* 1879, vol. XI. p. iv.

jointures and portions in favour of unborn or unascer-
tained persons, and subjected to every form of liability
in the way of easements, rent-charges or other burdens
in favour of adjoining owners and other persons[1]. Ever
since the great Civil War of the seventeenth century,
and especially during the present century, the practice
of settling land has continued to increase. It has
indeed become a national habit. When a man buys
land in England, it is very often at the end of a
successful mercantile career; he purchases a large
estate with the intention of founding a family; he
settles it either by his will or by deed, and thus the
complication begins. It was calculated in 1879 that
two-thirds of the land in England was in strict settlement, the title to a single estate being sometimes
vested in forty or fifty different persons, and the
"ownership" of the "limited owner" being little better
than a fiction[2]. So long as this condition of things
prevailed, every scheme for the registration of title
necessitated one of two things. Either (1) the interests
carved out of the original fee-simple must be placed on
the register (as was done by Lord Westbury's Act of
1862), a process which defeated the first object of the
registration of title, viz. simplicity of title for the
purposes of disposition. Or (2) an owner *pro hac vice*
must be created for the purpose of disposition, the
owners of particular estates and limited interests being

---

[1] *Parl. Pap.* 1879, vol. XI. p. iv.   (Report of Mr O. Morgan's
Committee.)

[2] John Tyrrell, *Evidence on Real Property*, p. 173; Osborne
Morgan's *Land Law Reform*, pp. 17 et seqq.; Joshua Williams'
Evidence before Mr O. Morgan's Committee, 1879, q. 409; Bartle
Frere's Evidence, *ibid.* q. 1287.

left to protect themselves by a system of cautions and inhibitions against the risk of having their property dealt with behind their backs; this was done by the Land Transfer Act of 1875[1]. In adopting the second alternative, Lord Cairns merely "removed from Lord Westbury's Register a specified number of estates and interests, and reproduced them in the shape of a number of specified persons whose consent to a transfer was necessary[2]." The operation of his Act was therefore necessarily hampered with regard to all settled land of which the title was split up among a number of persons each of whom was in a position, so to speak, to put a spoke in the wheel of a proposed transfer.

Whilst Lord Cairns' Land Transfer Act remained a dead letter, a number of sensational land-frauds took place. The worst of them were perpetrated by Dimsdale and Downes, each of whom by repeatedly mortgaging the same lands, obtained monies to the amount of ten to twenty times the aggregate value of the lands mortgaged[3]. This produced such feelings of alarm and insecurity in the public mind as to cause a renewed demand for some effective system of giving publicity to the transfer of land. Whether the public alarm was well-founded was a disputed question among conveyancers; some, perhaps exceptionally fortunate

[1] In practice cautions and inhibitions were found most unsatisfactory. They had either to be made so short as to afford hardly any protection, or so long as to impede very seriously the transfer of land, *vide* Joshua Williams' Evidence before Mr O. Morgan's Committee, *Parl. Pap.* 1879, vol. XI. q. 725.

[2] *Bar Committee's Report*, 25 March 1886, p. 51.

[3] Mr Learoyd's Evidence, *Parl. Pap.* 1878, XV. and 1879, XI. qq. 1621-4, and 1692 et seqq.

in their experience, contending that in sales of land frauds rarely if ever took place; while others spoke of their frequent occurrence. In mortgages, however, there was a general concurrence of opinion that frauds occurred often enough to render greater publicity desirable[1]. With regard to both purchasers and mortgagees it was further felt that such security as they enjoyed against fraud was generally due to their knowledge of the parties with whom they were dealing or to the character of the solicitor employed by them, rather than to the protection afforded by the law[2].

Under these circumstances the House of Commons in 1878 appointed a Select Committee to consider what steps should be taken to simplify the title to land, to facilitate its transfer and to prevent land-frauds. The Committee, commonly known as " Mr Osborne Morgan's Committee," took evidence during two sessions and presented an elaborate report in 1879[3]. The witnesses examined by the Committee ascribed the failure of the Land Transfer Act of 1875 to various causes. Some said it had failed because a title once registered could not be removed from the register. Others blamed the sinister interests of solicitors. Others, like Sir Henry Thring[4], thought that the breakdown of Lord Westbury's Act had " thrown a blight on the whole thing." The Committee themselves attributed the failure to the conservative character of Englishmen, their unwillingness to experiment with dangerous novelties,

---

[1] Joshua Williams' Evidence, *ubi sup.* qq. 666–673.

[2] *Parl. Pap.* 1879, vol. xi. p. vii.

[3] *Ibid.* 1878, xv. pp. 467 et seqq. ; 1879, xi. pp. 1–260.

[4] *Ubi sup.*, Evidence, q. 7.

their reverence for title-deeds, their preference for
managing their own affairs, their dislike of officialism,
their fear of detecting flaws in their own titles, and
what not[1]. With regard to the future of Registration
in England, the Committee found the position to stand
thus: On the one hand they were credibly informed[2]
that no system of registration of titles would be volun-
tarily accepted by the English public; on the other
hand they were told by Lord Chancellor Cairns that
he saw no way in which the registration of title
could be made compulsory[3]. The Committee therefore
despaired altogether of registration of title whether
optional or compulsory, although they hoped that it
would become possible at some vague future date when
the law of real property should have been sufficiently
amended and simplified. In the meantime, while in
the abstract preferring the registration of titles to
the registration of assurances, they proposed to guard
against land-frauds, such as those which had disturbed
the public mind, by introducing a compulsory registration of *assurances*. The proposal forms a curious
reversion to the scheme abandoned in 1853. Into its
details it is unnecessary to enter[4]. It was not acted
on, except in one particular. Under the proposed
registry, official searchers were to give certificates of
search to be used as evidence with regard to the
previous state of the title. This idea was soon after-

[1] *Parl. Pap.* 1879, xi. pp. iv et seqq.

[2] By Mr Follett, Registrar of the Irish Landed Estates Court, and
Mr Holt, Assistant Registrar under the Land Transfer Act.

[3] *Parl. Pap.* 1879, xi. p. vi.

[4] *Vide*, s. v., *Parl. Pap.* 1879, xi. pp. ix, xii et seqq.

wards applied to searches made in the Central office
of the Supreme Court; but without any marked degree
of success[1].

But while the Committee's main scheme fell to
the ground, their miscellaneous recommendations stand
next to those of the Real Property Commission in the
influence which they have exerted on the course of Real
Property legislation. Of these recommendations (which
aimed mainly at the simplification of title and the facilitation of land transfer) there is hardly one that has not
been adopted in actual legislation.

The Committee proposed, in the first place, to
make a real step towards cheapening and simplifying
conveyances, by altering the mode of payment of
solicitors. The matter was a standing nuisance of
ancient date. John Miller, John Tyrrell and Joshua
Williams had demonstrated that payment according
to length did not answer its proposed end of protecting the client against excessive charges, but, on the
contrary, that it increased expense ; that it discouraged
talent, promoted idleness, and tended to degrade a
liberal profession; that it gave to both solicitors and
conveyancing counsel a special interest adverse to
law-reform ; and that it inevitably caused ideas to
be expressed in far more words than was absolutely
necessary, and " diluted to their proper remunerating
strength[2]." The Royal Commission of 1854–7 had
expressed their strong disapproval of the system[3], but

---

[1] 45 & 46 Vict. c. 39, s. 2 ; 51 & 52 Vict. c. 51, s. 17; Elphinstone
and Clark on *Searches*, p. 166.

[2] Tyrrell, 1829, *Evidence etc.* p. 382 ; Miller on the *Civil Law*,
1825, p. 479 ; Joshua Williams, *The Transfer of Land*, p. 8.

[3] *Parl. Pap.* 1857, vol. xviii. p. 300 ; 1870, vol. xviii. p. xxxiii.

nothing was done till 1870, when the Land Transfer Commission procured the passing of an Act[1] giving some freedom of bargaining between solicitors and clients, and allowing officers taxing solicitors' costs to take into account the skill, labour and responsibility involved. This was an improvement, and deeds possibly became somewhat less verbose. But the evil was not cured. English deeds were still on an average ten times as long as Scottish deeds[2]; they were still, in Bentham's words, "oppressed with lengthiness, thence unintelligibility, expensiveness, dilatoriness." Clients complained, too, that they were practically at the mercy of their solicitors. In his evidence before Mr Osborne Morgan's Committee, 1879, Mr W. Farrer gave a remarkable case illustrating the uncertainty of solicitors' charges. Three ladies had employed three different solicitors to transact exactly the same business; the bill of the first was taxed at £18, that of the second at £17, that of the third at £223[3]. Mr Osborne Morgan's Committee proposed that a new scale of conveyancing charges should be adopted, arranged wherever possible upon a graduated *ad valorem* principle. This was done by the Solicitors' Remuneration Act of 1881[4], drafted by Lord Cairns. Under this Act, conveyancers' fees may still be fixed by private agreement, but otherwise they are regulated by a classified tariff, the scale of charges being calculated as a percentage on the value of the property dealt with.

[1] 33 & 34 Vict. c. 28.

[2] *Parl. Pap.* 1879, XI.; Mr Douglas' Evidence, q. 3374; Lord Cairns' Evidence, q. 2863.

[3] *Ibid.* p. viii.   [4] 44 & 45 Vict. c. 44.

Another expedient of Mr Osborne Morgan's Committee for curtailing deeds was to render obligatory the use of short statutory forms, like those used in Scotland, for the ordinary kinds of assurance, such as purchase deeds, mortgages, etc. Except in being compulsory, this suggestion proceeds on the same lines as Lord Brougham's Act of 1845 and Lord Cranworth's Act of 1859, the principle being to take for granted clauses which always appear in a deed. The outcome of this suggestion (though in an optional form) was the Conveyancing and Law of Property Act of 1881[1], drawn up by Lord Cairns with the aid of Mr Wolstenholme[2]. The provisions of this Act, so far as they aim at shortening and facilitating conveyances, are briefly as follows: It has made unnecessary the general words at the end of the "parcels" of a deed; in practice general words are now inserted only under special circumstances, and even then in an exceedingly condensed form[3]. It has likewise superseded the "all the estate" clause, which is now invariably omitted in practice. It has provided covenants for title, suitable for various forms of assurance, to be incorporated in deeds by the use of three or four statutory words; these also have been completely adopted into practice. It has also driven out of use covenants for the production of deeds, by substituting for them short written acknowledgments; has provided as alternative forms of limitation the words "in fee-simple" and "in tail";

[1] 44 & 45 Vict. c. 41; followed by the Conveyancing Act, 1882, 45 & 46 Vict. c. 39.

[2] *Parl. Pap.* 1895, xi., Lord Herschell, Evidence, q. 400.

[3] *Bar Committee's Report*, 5 March 1886, p. 8.

has rendered unnecessary the joint account clause in mortgages to trustees, and the insertion of powers of distress and entry in a grant of a rent-charge. With regard to mortgages, it has made it unnecessary to insert powers of sale, leasing, etc., in the mortgage deed, and such powers are now rarely inserted[1]. It has made an even greater improvement in providing for the sale of mortgaged land by the mortgager. Great difficulties had frequently arisen in selling land burdened with numerous charges. There were frequently to be found first mortgages on various independent portions of an estate; later mortgages comprising the land in these first mortgages and other land still unincumbered; and then later charges comprising the whole estate. In such cases the number of persons interested in the several mortgages was often very considerable; their united action was necessary to a sale of the property, but united action among a large number of persons could seldom take place, and sales of such properties were practically impossible without the aid of the Court[2]. But now by the Conveyancing Act of 1881, upon a sale of land subject to a mortgage lien or charge, payment may be made into Court of a sum sufficient to meet such incumbrances, and the Court may declare the land to be freed from the incumbrance. An owner of mortgaged land may thus convey an unincumbered fee-simple without the concurrence of the incumbrancers. When it is remembered that most of the land in

[1] Williams' *Conveyancing Statutes*, 141–4, 252–3.

[2] *Vide* Lawrence (President Incorporated Law Society), *Cambridge Address*, 1879, p. 26.

England is mortgaged, the degree in which this
provision facilitates land transfer will be realized.   To
the Act were appended certain schedules containing
short forms of mortgages, sales, marriage settlements,
etc., intended as models for conveyances under the
general provisions of the Act.   In simple cases of the
kinds of transactions to which they refer, these forms
have obtained a considerable currency in practice[1].
It is convenient to notice here with regard to settlement deeds in particular, that they have been reduced
to a fraction of their former length by the Settled Land
Act of 1882[2], which has rendered superfluous the
cumbrous powers of sale, leasing and exchange, formerly
vested in the trustees of the settlement.   With regard to
contracts for the sale of land, finally, the Conveyancing
Act, 1881[3], besides endeavouring to supersede express
conditions of sale, has curtailed the rights of purchasers
on *open* contracts in several minor points, in order to
save expense to the vendor.

The Solicitors' Remuneration Act and the Conveyancing Acts are important pieces of legislation.
But the most valuable, we may almost say the epoch-
making, conclusion to which Mr Osborne Morgan's
Committee came, was that "to legislate for the
registration of titles without as a preliminary step
simplifying the titles to be registered, was to begin
at the wrong end"; that is to say, in the words of
their chairman, "before transfer can be simple, title

[1] *Bar Committee's Report*, 25 March 1886, pp. 8, 12.

[2] 45 & 46 Vict. c. 38, to be more fully noticed later.   *Infra*, p. 62.

[3] 44 & 45 Vict. c. 41, s. 3, amending the Vendor and Purchaser
Act, 1874 (37 & 38 Vict. c. 78, s. 2).

must become simple. The right to deal with the land must be gathered up into one or two hands, and not split up among a large number of persons[1]." The Committee, in short, were convinced that the main cause of the difficulties of land transfer was the prevalent practice of settling or entailing land; and while realizing that such a change would run counter to public sentiment, they strongly recognized the expediency of limiting the power of settlement. This could be done, they declared, *either* by prohibiting the owner of property from tying it up and charging it, except in a particular manner; *or* by giving to the possessory proprietor the right of dealing with the land as if it was his own. We shall see that the second alternative has for the present been chosen by Parliament, but that events appear to be moving towards the adoption of the first.

Settlements of land have for many years formed a political bone of contention, and they are at the present day widely attacked as being the principal obstacle to the diffusion of land amongst small owners. The procedure of settlement is familiar to lawyers. A landowner on marriage or majority obtains a life-estate only, with remainder in tail to his eldest and other sons in succession, and in default of sons, to his daughters in tail. When the eldest son comes of age, the father (tenant for life in possession) obtains the cooperation of the said son (tenant in tail in remainder) to bar the entail; the father is in a position

---

[1] *Parl. Pap.* 1879, xi. p. vi; Osborne Morgan, *Land Law Reform*, p. 11.

to bring strong pressure to bear, and the land is re-settled on the said son for life, with remainders in tail to his unborn sons in succession. In each succeeding generation the process is repeated. In each case the settlement contains charges in favour of widows and younger children, and it often happens that an estate is burdened with family charges in favour of three co-existing generations of widows and younger children.

The vitality of the custom is justly ascribed by Bentham to three causes; the first is the desire of preventing prodigality, the second is family pride, joined to "that agreeable illusion which paints the successive existence of our descendants as the pro-longation of our own," and the third is the love of power, the desire of ruling after death[1]. Many are the evils attributed to the system, and it is a point to be remembered that its wide prevalence adds weight to any well-founded complaints against it. It would not be surprising if a system under which land is held by a succession of impecunious life-tenants should give rise to many inconveniences. On the contrary, it is every day being more strongly realized that if the "owner" of land has too limited an estate, he cannot deal with his property in the manner most beneficial either for himself, his family, or the community at large[2]. Of the evils thus arising, many are bound up with the shortcomings of our rural system above described; those which more directly inhere in the practice of settlement may be divided under four heads.

---

[1] *Theory of Legislation*, transl. Hildreth, Part II. chap. II.

[2] Cf. the Lord Chancellor in Hansard, IIIrd series, CXXXVIII. p. 397.

In the first place, settlements give to the owner of an estate only a life interest, and they curtail even his life income by endless charges in favour of all manner of persons born and unborn. They thus reduce both his ability and his inclination to make permanent improvements on the property and to promote the welfare of the agricultural population. He has no interest in making improvements involving a large outlay on which he can expect no adequate return during his own life; he cannot even raise money by mortgaging the property beyond his own life interest. Mill's evidence on this point is particularly emphatic. "It cannot be said," he wrote[1], "that the English landed proprietor is generally an improver of land.... The truth is that any very general improvement of land by the landlord is incompatible with a law or *custom* of primogeniture. When the land goes wholly to the heir, it generally goes to him severed from the pecuniary resources which would enable him to improve it, the personal property being absorbed by the provision for younger children and the land itself often heavily burdened for the same purpose. Few landlords can therefore make expensive improvements without borrowing money and adding to the mortgages with which their land is already burdened. But the position of the owner of a deeply mortgaged estate is so precarious, economy so unwelcome to one whose apparent fortune greatly exceeds his real means, that it is no

---

[1] *Political Economy*, Book II. ch. II. §§ 5, 6. In the English rural system it is of course the landlord by whom permanent improvements are executed (if at all), neither the tenant nor the labourer being in a position to do so.

wonder if few landlords find themselves in a condition to make immediate sacrifices for the sake of future profit."

This class of evils it has been attempted to mitigate by several Statutes of the Queen's reign, intended to stimulate the application of capital to land in settlement. An Act of 1845[1] empowered life-tenants to make drainage improvements and to charge the expense, with the consent of Chancery, on the inheritance of the land. Advances of public money for this purpose were provided for by the " Public Money Drainage Acts[2]." By the " Private Money Drainage Act " of 1849 tenants for life were empowered to borrow money for drainage improvements with the aid of the five Land Improvement Companies[3], the money being repayable by a twenty-two years' rent-charge. The principle was extended to other permanent improvements by the Improvement of Land Act of 1864[4], and tenants for life were authorized to borrow money without the aid of the Land Improvement Companies. The list of improvements was made to include mansion-houses by the Limited Owners' Residences Act of 1870[5], and reservoirs and watersupply works by the Limited Owners' Reservoirs and Watersupply further Facilities Act of 1877[6]. The list of improvements has again been extended and provision has been made for the applica-

---

[1] 8 & 9 Vict. c. 56, repealing 3 & 4 Vict. c. 55.

[2] 9 & 10 Vict. c. 101 ; 10 & 11 Vict. c. 119 ; 13 & 14 Vict. c. 31 ; 19 & 20 Vict. c. 9.

[3] 12 & 13 Vict. c. 100; 19 & 20 Vict. c. 9.

[4] 27 & 28 Vict. c. 114.

[5] 33 & 34 Vict. c. 56. amended by 34 & 35 Vict. c. 84.

[6] 40 & 41 Vict. c. 31.

tion of capital, money arising under the Acts, by the various Settled Land Acts. None of these Acts have been very successful. In 1873 Lord Salisbury reported, as chairman of a Select Committee, that "although considerable use had been made of the Improvement Acts, the progress had not been so rapid as was desirable, and what had been accomplished was only a small portion of what still remained to be done"; and Mr Caird estimated of all kinds of improvements that only one-fifth had been accomplished of what required to be done. More recently Mr Shaw Lefevre declares, "Some good has been effected under the Improvement Acts, but the system is applicable rather to the larger estates which can bear the cost of obtaining the approval of the Land Department. The Acts, though beneficial, have not succeeded in making any great impression on the amount of improvement which might be effected on entailed estates[1]."

The second drawback of the practice of settlement is that it renders land inalienable, prevents it from coming into the hands best fitted to turn it to profit, prevents the owner from raising money by selling parts of his estate, and prevents the diffusion of land among small farmers, shopkeepers and peasants[2]. At Common Law, too, the life-tenant could not grant leases longer than the duration of his own interest, which rendered the tenure of farmers insecure, and frequently prevented desirable building or mining leases. These disadvantages were much lessened by the practice, already common in the beginning of the century, of inserting

[1] *Agrarian Tenures*, ch. III. (1893 A.D.).

[2] *Vide* Kay, *Free Trade in Land*, pp. 59 et seqq.

powers of leasing and sale in settlements[1]. But the practice was not invariable. Powers were often accidentally omitted, particularly powers of sale and exchange and of building and mining leases. Until the year 1856 such omissions had to be remedied in each particular case by private Acts of Parliament, at an average annual cost of £17,000[2]. To obviate the expense and inconvenience of this procedure, an Act[3] was passed in 1856 directing tenants for life to apply to the Court of Chancery instead of to Parliament in all cases where powers of leasing and sale were omitted from settlements, provided that the settlement contained no declaration expressly forbidding such application, and provided that the consent had been obtained of a number of specified persons interested in the land, including the person for the time being in whom the remainder in tail was vested. The Act was amended by the Settled Estates Acts[4] of 1858, of 1864, of 1874, of 1876 and of 1877. By the last the consent of the Chancery Division was for some leases rendered unnecessary; and for mining, building and repairing leases the Court was empowered to dispense with the consent of interested parties in certain cases where such consent is unimportant or difficult to obtain. But all these Acts could be excluded by a declaration in the settlement. They remedied the difficulties caused by the accidental omission of powers of leasing

[1] John Tyrrell, *Evidence*, pp. 139 et seqq.

[2] The Lord Chancellor in Hansard, cxxxviii. pp. 397 et seqq.

[3] Settled Estates Act, 1856, 19 & 20 Vict. c. 120.

[4] 21 & 22 Vict. c. 77; 27 & 28 Vict. c. 45; 37 & 38 Vict. c. 33; 39 & 40 Vict. c. 30; 40 & 41 Vict. c. 38.

and sale, but they did not meet the inconveniences
arising through their express exclusion, nor did they
touch the difficulties of restricted or ill-devised powers.
Such powers as were inserted in deeds of settlement
were usually given to the trustees of the settlement,
and not to the tenant for life, and it was found in
practice that trustees having powers were more anxious
to act with safety, and, as far as possible, with freedom
from responsibility, than to engage in any exercise of
those powers. It was also found that the powers
inserted in settlements were frequently inadequate to
provide for the due improvement of the land; with
regard to the power of sale in particular, no settlement ever authorized its trustees to sell the estate and
convert it into money in the very case in which it was
most desirable that the land should be so converted,
viz. when the tenant for life was of opinion that it did
not suit his taste or capacity to manage landed estate.
In such cases, even if the trustees had a power of sale,
the proceeds of the sale were usually required to be
invested in other land[1].

In order to remedy these defects of settlements, and
probably also in order to render practicable his own
system of registration of title, Lord Cairns adopted the
second alternative indicated by Mr Osborne Morgan's
Committee. In 1880 and the two succeeding years he
introduced a Settled Land Bill. In 1882 he declared
that if the bill became law "it would for every good
purpose place the limited owner of property in the
same position in which the owner of the fee-simple
stood; it would lead to the execution of improvements

[1] *Vide* Lord Cairns in 1882, Hansard, ccLxvi. pp. 1076 et seqq.

in land as if the land were owned in fee-simple, and it would lead to the more easy and free circulation of land[1]." The bill was submitted to the Royal Commission on Agricultural Interests, which reported that "the ample powers which it conferred upon life-tenants would obviate many of the objections which had been urged against the existing system of English land-laws[2]." The bill became the Settled Land Act of 1882[3]. The Act limits the settlor's capacity of controlling the future fate of his property. The powers of leasing, sale and exchange defined by the Act are inalienably and indefeasibly vested in every sort of beneficial limited owner known to the law (except tenants in dower and mere leaseholders at a rent)[4], and are vested directly in the tenant for life (or other limited owner) and not in the trustees of the settlement, although the consent of the latter or of the Chancery Division is required for dealings with the mansion-house and its grounds. Money derived from the sale of land under the Act is paid not to the limited owner but to the trustees or the Court, and may by them be invested in authorized securities. With regard to the application of the Act, it has been calculated[5] that only a minute fraction of the land in England and Wales is excluded from the powers conferred by it, this minute fraction consisting of land held in right of dower and land subject to unusual or eccentric trusts rarely occurring in practice.

[1] Lord Cairns, *ubi sup.*

[2] *Parl. Pap.* 1882, vol. xiv. p. 29.

[3] 45 & 46 Vict. c. 38.   [4] *Ibid.* s. 58.

[5] *Vide Report of Bar Committee*, 25 March 1886, pp. 15, 16.

The main principle of this masterly piece of legislation is that the limited owner in possession for the
time being is the Agent for the whole group of persons
entitled under the settlement[1]. His powers of disposition are given him for the general benefit of the whole
group.   The limited owner has the initiative, the
Court and the trustees have a supervising control.
The grand effect of the Act has been to make land
in settlement as easily transferable, so far as legal
capacity is concerned, as land held in fee-simple.
From this statement there must, however, be excepted
the mansion-house and its grounds, which are still
subject to some restraints.   In practice some use has
been made of the powers conferred by the Act, but
sales of settled land have not been so numerous as
they were expected to be.   In the main there can be
no doubt that this disappointing result is due to the
vitality of the custom of keeping family estates in the
family.   Perhaps, however, Lord Herschell is right in
blaming the restraints on the alienation of the mansion-
house and grounds[2]; probably, also, Mr Shaw Lefevre
partially accounts for the disappointment by referring
to the limited scope for the investment of the proceeds
of sale of settled land, and to the agricultural depression
which began in 1879 and which has greatly lowered
the market value of land[3].

Besides impeding the diffusion of land and the
application of capital to land, settlements have had a
third evil effect of a more general nature.   By making

[1] 45 & 46 Vict. c. 38, s. 53.
[2] Hansard, 1887, cccxiii. p. 1767.
[3] *Agrarian Tenures*, p. 43.

the title to English land complex and intricate to an extreme degree, they have increased the expense of its transfer and the insecurity of its possession. With regard to settled land itself the Settled Land Act of 1882 has in this respect effected much improvement. A purchaser of settled land has now no need to trouble himself about charges, jointures, portions, special powers of appointment, remainders, or any interests subsequent to the estate of the limited owner in possession[1]. The conveyance by the latter *ipso jure* discharges the land from all the intricacies of the settlement, and from all estates subsisting or to arise thereunder. But it is maintained by the most experienced lawyers that ease and cheapness of transfer will never be attained in England while the landowner keeps his power of creating intricate and often superfluous interests in his land. Perhaps however the national habit is too strong for the law; Mr Osborne Morgan's Committee indeed wished to " impress the fact that in a country like England simplicity of title is more or less unattainable[2]." We shall recur to the subject.

The fourth and last class of evils to which settlements give rise is mainly of a domestic nature. Joseph Kay, Mill, and others have described how the heir of entail is rendered to a great extent independent of his father ; " being assured of succeeding to the family property, however undeserving of it, and being aware of this from his earliest years, he has much more than the ordinary chances of growing up idle, dissipated and profligate." The settlement also makes the landowner

---

[1] 45 & 46 Vict. c. 38, s. 20.
[2] *Parl. Pap.* 1879, vol. xi. p. vii.

careless about the education of the child who is to
succeed to the ownership of the estate, because he
knows that the son, whatever his extravagance or folly,
cannot lose or lessen the estates or the social status of
the family[1]. These attributes of settlements have not
been touched by the Settled Land Act of 1882. The
son is still independent of the father. The father
can indeed under the Act convert the land into other
forms of property, but of their value he cannot deprive
the son.

It appears, then, on the whole, that the various
disadvantages of settlements have been only very
partially removed by the Land Improvement Acts
and the Settled Land Acts; and many law-reformers
have proposed more substantial limitations on the
power of settlement.

The proposal which promises to be first adopted by
law is that of abolishing estates tail either altogether
or as soon as the tenant in tail comes of age. It is
obvious that the conversion of estates tail into fee-
simple estates would hardly affect the present powers
of the tenant in tail in possession; but it would enable
tenants in tail in remainder to dispose of their interests
without the consent of the tenant for life or other
"protector of the settlement." At present the utmost
that a tenant in tail in remainder can do without such
consent is to create a base fee, and base fees cause
enormous difficulty and expense in land transfer; conveyancers describe them as "the most odious things

[1] Kay, *Free Trade in Land*, pp. 48 et seqq.; Mill, *Political Economy*,
Bk. v. ch. ix. § 3.

that one can have to deal with[1]." Bills to abolish
estates tail were introduced in 1877, 1878 and 1882.
In 1887 Lord Halsbury's Land Transfer Bill proposed
with regard to estates tail that whenever a person of
full age should have power without the consent of any
one else to enlarge his estate tail by deed duly enrolled,
then the law should do it for him; that estates tail
should not be created for the future, and that the
Statute of Westminster II. should be repealed. The
proposal was approved of by Lord Selborne and Lord
Herschell, but it shared the fate of the rest of the
Land Transfer Bill[2]. The change, when it takes place,
will be a small one, but in the right direction; it will
have little effect on the tying up of land, but it will
simplify title and form a step towards the assimilation
of Real and Personal Property.

Some law-reformers, however, would go further.
Mr Shaw Lefevre's scheme, supported by Lord Herschell,
Sir Julian Goldsmid, Mr Osborne Morgan, and others[3],
is to render void all remainders to unborn persons
other than remainders to the children of the tenant for
life in such proportion as he may appoint, and in
default of appointment, equally among the children.
This proposal, which was embodied in bills of 1877
and 1878, would certainly remove the domestic
grievances of settlements to which we have alluded; it
would give the father control over the son. But it

[1] *Parl. Pap.* 1879, vol. xi., Mr Bartle Frere, Evidence, qq. 1165–86;
Mr Young, Evidence, qq. 1421–36.

[2] Hansard, cccxiii. pp. 27, 32, 1767.

[3] Osborne Morgan, *Land Law Reform*, p. 29; Hansard, vol.
cccxiii. p. 1767.

may be doubted whether it would seriously diminish the facilities now existing for the tying up of land and the complicating of title.

Others there are who would completely abolish settlements by making void all estates whatsoever to unborn persons. Their standpoint is that since the complication of title and the accumulation of land is demonstrably due to the system of entail which has existed in England for two centuries, the obvious remedy is to abolish that system. They consider that England should do now what other nations have done long ago, and should reverse the influence of its legislation instead of giving the utmost facilities for tying up the land. They declare that although the Settled Land Act gives to the limited owner the *legal capacity* to sell his land, land was not, even before the passing of that Act, tied up by any bond of legal incapacity, but by the *custom* of settlement and re-settlement; and that the Act does hardly anything to discourage that custom. It is true, they say, that the abolition of settlements of land would place the owner of land in this respect in an inferior position to the owner of personal property, and would introduce a new distinction between the two species of property; but this distinction would be an expedient one, it would be one of the few expedient distinctions which can be drawn between moveable and immoveable property; to Mill it seemed " almost an axiom that property in *land* should be interpreted strictly, and that the balance in all cases of doubt should incline against the proprietor[1],"

[1] *Political Economy*, Bk. II. ch. II. § 5.

for no man made the land. The question is naturally
one on which the two great political parties have taken
opposite sides. Conservative statesmen have shown
themselves strongly opposed to all attempted meddling
with settlements. Thus Lord Halsbury in 1887 announced his determination to leave untouched the
power of settlement[1]; while Lord Salisbury stoutly
maintained that "the abolition of settlements would
not promote the diffusion of land ; it might produce a
greater diffusion of land among proprietors of a more
moderate size, but it would have no effect at all on the
diffusion of land among the people whose possession of
it would give it a real political security, and it was
very doubtful to his mind whether it would produce
any diffusion at all. If, as he believed, the tendency of
land would always be to get itself into few hands—
because land was an unremunerative investment, and
must therefore, to a certain extent, be the investment
of rich men—for that reason, the more they made it
easy for land to pass from hand to hand, the more they
might expect it on the whole to get into fewer hands[2]."
As we have seen, Parliament as a whole has subsequently
adopted a more pronounced policy in favour of the
diffusion of rural land. So far as an ideal for the
future English rural system can be extracted from the
conflicting views of political parties, it is one in which
large and small ownerships will exist side by side, the
large landed proprietor being the guide, philosopher
and politician of the enlightened and independent
peasant owners clustering round his estate. How far

[1] Hansard, vol. cccxiii. p. 27.   [2] *Ibid.* cccxiii. p. 1770.

this ideal can be attained by legislation is a most disputable question. The Acts so far passed with this purpose, giving to local authorities powers for forming small holdings, are of doubtful success, and avowedly experimental[1]. If they should definitely fail, and if the legislature should be and remain earnestly bent on re-creating a class of small landowners, settlements will probably be abolished and perhaps in the far future some system of compulsory division of inheritances introduced.

We may now resume the history of the registration of title. After the great law-reforms which had been initiated by Mr Osborne Morgan's Committee, it was in 1887 considered that titles had been sufficiently simplified to justify another attempt at introducing their compulsory registration. In that year Lord Halsbury introduced a bill for the compulsory registration of title. The bill proposed to enable possessory titles to be under certain circumstances converted into absolute titles, to create a Realty Representative, and to provide for the establishment of an insurance fund. Its compulsory clauses required every person to place his title on the register before selling, settling, or mortgaging his land, and provided that on the death of a landowner his successor in title should not acquire any legal rights until the land had been registered. The bill came to grief in the House of Commons. It was re-introduced in 1888, and was referred to a Select Committee, which considered the bill during the sessions of 1888 and 1889. In the latter year it was defeated in the House of Lords, evidently on

[1] *Vide* Hansard, ivth series, vol. i. p. 911 (1892).

account of certain provisions which it contained concerning primogeniture; and Lord Halsbury gave up the struggle. It was resumed by Lord Herschell in 1893, but his Registration Bill reached the Commons too late in the session to be passed. It was reintroduced in 1894, but was postponed until after the passing of the Finance Act of that year. In 1895 Lord Herschell brought it in again. In the House of Commons it was referred to a Select Committee, which examined many witnesses. Lord Herschell, in his evidence, defended the compulsory registration of title on the old ground that it would dispense with the repetition of tedious investigation on each successive conveyance of the same land; and he maintained that registration of title would not, as was alleged, increase the opportunities for fraud and forgery[1]. Much evidence was given by solicitors, tending to show that the existing law charges for small transactions in land were extremely low, and that registration of title would increase rather than diminish the cost of small transactions[2]. In 1897 the bill was again introduced by Lord Halsbury, and passed into law. The " Land Transfer Act, 1897 " is now on probation in certain districts of England, and nothing can as yet be said with certainty as to its future operation or chances of success.

Before leaving the subject of land transfer, we have to notice a peculiar restriction on the alienation

---

[1] *Parl. Pap.* 1895, vol. xi., Lord Herschell's Evidence, qq. 15, 67.

[2] *Ibid.* Mr Wolstenholme's Evidence, qq. 454–60; and tables of charges in Appendix.

of land which has recently formed a subject of legislation; we have to give a brief account of charitable uses[1].

Restraints were imposed on the donation of land to charities by the "Statute of Mortmain" of 1736[2], a legislative oddity in every way. The objects and purposes enumerated in the preamble of the Act (viz. to prevent the disherison of lawful heirs, to prevent charitable donations by languishing or dying persons, etc.) are altogether inadequate to account for the provisions which follow. It seems probable that the Act owed its birth to passing causes of a merely party character; it may have been intended as a side-thrust at certain "Jacobites and Dissenters[3]." However this may be, the Act does most shrewdly discourage gifts of land to charitable uses. It provides that no gift of land, or of any interest in land, or of personal estate to be laid out in the purchase of land, shall be valid unless made *inter vivos*, absolutely, irrevocably, and with immediate transfer of possession. The framers of the Act knew how to operate on the self-interest of men; they saw that "the more absolute a gift was required to be, the less was the chance of a man having the generosity to make it[4]." The other requirements of the Statute, such as the presence of witnesses and the inrolment of the deed in Chancery, are obvious precautions to secure publicity and, at need, evidence

---

[1] Our account will be all the more brief, as the subject has been fully treated by Prof. C. S. Kenny in his *Endowed Charities*.

[2] 9 Geo. II. c. 36.

[3] *Vide* Kenny, *Endowed Charities*, p. 61; Lord Herschell in 1891, Hansard, cccliv. p. 714.

[4] Kenny, *Endowed Charities*, p. 108.

of the donor's mental condition and of the genuineness
of the gift.

Many inconveniences have been caused by the
sweeping character of the restraints imposed by the
Statute. In their anxiety to ensure that gifts of land
to charities, if made at all, should be genuine and
absolute, the legislators of 1736 have inflicted on
charities several unintended hardships. It was found
in practice, for example, that the Statute made it
impossible to give land to charities without giving
also the minerals under the land, and that it disabled
charities from even *buying* land in districts where
sellers declined to sell except for a perpetual or other
rent-charge[1]. These difficulties were to some extent
removed by an Act of 1861[2], which provided that gifts
of land to charity should not be void by reason only
of containing certain reservations in favour of the
donor, such as a nominal rent, or provisions for the
better enjoyment of the property granted as well as
of adjacent property; and by an Act of 1864[3], which
allowed the consideration for a sale of land to a charity
to consist of a substantial rent. Even more serious
grievances were caused by the prohibition of "all
estates and interests whatsoever in land." These words,
probably in the first instance wider than the intention
of the legislature, gave an opening for a still wider
judicial interpretation, an enormous amount of litigation, and much disappointment of expectation. Judges,
even while acknowledging that the charitable donations

---

[1] Kenny, *Endowed Charities*, p. 108.

[2] 24 Vict. c. 9, amended by 25 & 26 Vict. c. 17.

[3] 27 & 28 Vict. c. 13, s. 4.

which they prevented were by no means within the
mischief of the Statute, persisted in what looked very
much like a crusade against private bounty, and continued to draw " distinctions which nobody could call
other than absurd." It has been decided, for example,
that a benevolent testator may not bequeath money
secured upon mortgage; that he may bequeath bonds
of the Corporation of Dewsbury and Wakefield, because
they are not interests in land, but that he may not
bequeath bonds of the Corporation of Salford and
Oldham, because they are interests in land; that he
may bequeath East India Stock, but not Metropolitan
Board of Works Consolidated Stock[1]. During the
course of the present century the Statute of Mortmain
has been relaxed in particular cases, according as one
charitable institution or another appeared to the legislature to be specially worthy of encouragement. The
inevitable consequence has been worse confusion and
uncertainty in the minds of testators, and the failure
of numberless beneficial bequests[2].

It has remained to the present day the policy of the
law to discourage gifts of land to charities. The policy
does not arise out of any general hostility to private
bounty; on the contrary, the law regards charities with
peculiar favour. Private bounty is, of course, in general
a most commendable thing; it is a thing to be fostered
and cherished; it is only discouraged in the particular
case in which it takes the form of a gift of land, because
in that particular case the disadvantages are considered
to outweigh the advantages. Land held from genera-

[1] *Vide* Lord Herschell in 1891, Hansard, CCCLIV. p. 713.
[2] *Ibid.* For a list of privileged charities, *v.* Jarman, *Wills*, 202–4.

tion to generation for charitable uses has ever tended
and still tends to remain out of the market and inalienable[1]. Another serious economic disadvantage of
charity land has recently emerged ; it has been proved
that land held by charities is as a rule administered
in a most unprofitable manner, and that the absence
of enlightened self-interest and the opportunities for
jobbery and abuse of patronage have made land a bad
investment even from the point of view of the charities
themselves[2]. For these reasons, and also because of
the growing demand for the distribution of land among
many owners, the policy of the legislature has been
strengthened rather than weakened in a sense adverse
to the locking-up of land in charity; and the many
attempts which have been made during the Queen's
reign to reverse this policy have been unsuccessful[3].
At the same time it has been realized more and more
strongly that the balance of utility usually lies on the
side of permitting private bounty, and that in the case
of *land* only, in the strict sense of the term, does the
balance lie the other way. The ideal of legislation
would, therefore, be to maintain the freedom of land
without discouraging private bounty ; to permit private
bounty without locking up land in charity.

A method of attaining this ideal was in 1861
indicated by the Committee of the Law Amendment

[1] Lord Herschell, Hansard, cccLv. pp. 318 et seqq. For the action
of the Charity Commissioners in this respect, *vide* Kenny on *Endowed
Charities*, pp. 96–7.

[2] Kenny, *Endowed Charities*, pp. 81–7.

[3] For an account of these attempts, *vide* Kenny, *Endowed Charities*,
passim, pp. 56–131 ; and Lord Herschell in Hansard, cccLiv. pp. 713
et seqq.

Society; they proposed that gifts of land to charities should be permitted as freely as gifts of money, but that the land should be prevented from reaching the charitable institution *in the shape of land* by requiring all lands so given or devised (except such sites or plots as might be necessary for the institution founded) to be sold or converted into money within a definite period of time[1]. The proposal was almost literally carried out in a bill introduced by Lord Herschell in 1891. This bill met with some opposition, chiefly on the ground that the compulsory sale of lands given to charity would "deprive charities of the unearned increment which they undoubtedly deserved to obtain[2]"; but it passed both Houses, and became the "Mortmain and Charitable Uses Act Amendment Act[3]" of 1891[4]. The Act provides that land may be given by will to any charitable use, but land so given is required to be sold within one year from the testator's death; the Act has also removed the restrictions on gifts of money and other personal estate "savouring of the realty," and permits testamentary gifts of personal estate directed to be laid out in the purchase of land for charitable uses, but the property bequeathed is to be held by the charity as if there had been no direction to lay

[1] Kenny, *Endowed Charities*, p. 94.

[2] Hansard, cccliv. p. 719, and ccclv. p. 316. For an examination of this argument, *vide* Kenny, *Endowed Charities*, pp. 87 et seqq.

[3] 54 & 55 Vict. c. 73.

[4] The "Mortmain and Charitable Uses Act" of 1888 (51 & 52 Vict. c. 42), which substantially re-enacted the Statute of Mortmain, was a purely consolidating Statute prepared by the Statute Law Reform Commission, *vide* Hansard, cccxxii. p. 1597.

it out in the purchase of land. The law of charitable donations has thus been placed on a reasonable footing. The alienability of land is preserved without restraining private beneficence; the charity receives the value of the gift, and the land is left free to be applied to other better and more suitable uses.

CHAPTER III

TENURES AND THEIR INCIDENTS.

THE Real Property Commissioners in their third report drew a large distinction between *Tenure* and *Tenures*.

With regard to tenure, they had deeply considered the question whether it would be advisable to abolish the rule, fiction or principle of law which vests the absolute property or *dominium directum* of all lands in the Crown, and which supposes all lands in the hands of a subject to be held of some superior by virtue of an original grant[1]. But they felt no hesitation in recommending that the fiction should be retained. Most of the inconvenient restrictions and oppressive incidents of tenure had been taken away in 1660 by St. 12 Car. II. c. 24. On the other hand the consequences of tenure still pervaded the whole system of our Real Property Law so deeply and extensively, that its

[1] *Third Report*, p. 323. Many persons of great learning (*e.g.* James Humphreys, *Real Property*, p. 180) had proposed that all lands should be held in absolute or allodial ownership by their immediate owners.

abolition would be a dangerous and unpractical inno-
vation; it would become necessary immediately to
provide by positive legislation for all the rules deduced
from the principle of tenure, and the Commissioners
feared that some of these rules would escape attention
notwithstanding the greatest care, that many questions
would arise upon the meaning of the terms in which
the existing law would be declared, and that all the
dangers and evils of codification would be encountered
without its advantages. The principle of tenure still
subsists. It is recognized indeed that the abolition of
the venerable fiction would remove a most artificial
distinction between real and personal property; the
distinction moreover is an unnecessary one, for, it is
hardly necessary to say, its abolition would leave intact
the "eminent domain" of the Sovereign, including its
right of expropriation and its rights as *ultimus heres*.
The general feeling about the matter nevertheless is
that it is "not worth while." Some advanced politicians with leanings towards the municipalization or
nationalization of the land even regard the fiction with
positive affection, as indicating, in a symbolic manner,
the principle that property in land and property in
moveables are to be differently construed.

While acquiescing in the principle of tenure, the
Real Property Commissioners regarded as an unqualified
and purposeless evil the variety of *tenures* existing in
England[1]. They declared that this variety of tenures
afforded one of the many instances in which laws had
been retained where the circumstances under which

---

[1] *Third Report*, pp. 326 et seqq.

they originated were entirely altered; that the variety of tenures afforded no facilities either for varying the modes in which land might be occupied, or for enabling the owner to regulate the succession to it; that the positive evils arising from it were therefore wholly uncompensated. These evils were, first, that the variety of different systems of property law to be administered by the same tribunals made it impossible for practitioners and even for judges, however carefully selected, to know and remember the law; secondly, that it was almost impossible to adapt measures meant for the improvement of the law of Real Property, to the various existing tenures; lastly, that the variety of tenures often greatly increased the expense of land transfer; the same field, or the site of the same house, being sometimes partly copyhold and partly freehold, and the purchaser being therefore compelled to examine two titles and execute two sets of conveyances.

The tenures which existed then are the same as those which exist at the present day, viz. Free and Common Socage, Socage subject to the customs of Gavelkind and Borough-English, the two Spiritual Tenures, Tenure by Grand Sergeanty, Tenure of Ancient Demesne, and Copyhold Tenure. Of these, Free and Common Socage is of course the ordinary tenure, and all the rest may be considered peculiar. Of the peculiar tenures, again, Copyholds are the most widely diffused throughout the country; the others are of minor importance.

With regard to the two Spiritual Tenures (Frankalmoigne and by Divine Service) the Real Property Commissioners thought that they might safely be preserved

as being harmless and presenting no inconvenience[1].
Grand Sergeanty, again, is held by honorary services
which, instead of being burdensome, are the source of
some distinction and profit to the owners of estates.
As these services do not interfere with the transmission
or the enjoyment of the estate and give rise to no
litigation, the Commissioners thought it " rather desirable that they should be preserved, as illustrating the
history and the antiquities of the country[2]." The tenure
of Ancient Demesne presented some inconveniences.
In certain cases land held by this tenure could not be
recovered or conveyed except by proceedings in the
Manor Court, and titles were often rendered unmarketable in consequence of fines and recoveries of such land
being levied and suffered in the Court of Common
Pleas at Westminster. The Commissioners recommended that the tenure should be abolished, or at
least that the fines and recoveries should be abolished[3].
By the Act for the Abolition of Fines and Recoveries[4]
it was provided that a simple deed should be substituted for the fines and recoveries of land held in
Ancient Demesne, and a Statute of 1852[5] provided
that actions for the recovery of such land should be
brought in the ordinary law-courts. The tenure now
presents no inconveniences.

Of Gavelkind land the most substantial peculiarity
is its law of descent, which is neither that of primogeniture nor of equal partibility. The descent of
gavelkind land is in reality usually controlled by wills

---

[1] *Third Report*, p. 327.   [2] *Ibid.* p. 327.
[3] *Ibid.* p. 332.   [4] 3 & 4 Will. IV. c. 74, ss. 4–6.
[5] 15 & 16 Vict. c. 76, s. 168.

and settlements, which would seem to show that its law
of intestacy does not peculiarly suit the inclinations or
the necessities of gavelkind tenants.   When the gavelkind law of intestacy *does* come into operation, it often
gives rise to great inconveniences ; thus no sale or
lease of the inherited estate can be made until the
youngest son can execute a conveyance ; titles are
rendered intricate and transfer impeded on account of
the subdivision of the land, especially in the descent
of trust estates.   Difficulties also arise in ascertaining
which lands are gavelkind and which have been dis-
gavelled[1].   The Real Property Commissioners proposed
to abolish the tenure, but it still exists.   Many attempts
have been made to abolish it, but it is in a peculiarly
strong position to resist reform; while gavelkind tenants
cherish it for the sake of its past benefits, law-reformers
vaguely realize that in some of its incidents it is superior
to the ordinary law.

The custom of Borough-English has also been found
to give rise to some inconveniences.   It certainly cannot
be supported by any of the arguments which favour
gavelkind, and it causes both delay and insecurity in
the deduction of title, on account of the difficulty of
obtaining in a given case satisfactory evidence that
there has not been more than a stated number of sons,
or that there has not been a son younger than the son
in question ; and it is sometimes difficult, especially in
Surrey, to ascertain whether the custom does or does
not extend to collateral relations[2].   The Real Property

---

[1] *Real. Prop. Comm. Third Report*, p. 329.

[2] *Ibid.* p. 328.

Commissioners recommended that the custom should be abolished, but it is still in existence.

Copyhold tenure, which is in itself the most inconvenient, and which contains within itself the most perplexing variety of customs, is also the most widely extended of the peculiar tenures. From a very early period complaint has been made against copyholds, and regret has frequently been expressed that they were not included in the great alteration which was made in the law of tenures in the reign of Charles II. Shortly after this change took place, Roger North observed that " it was somewhat unequal when the parliament took away the Royal tenures in capite, that the lesser tenures of the gentry were left exposed to as grievous abuses as the former[1]." It is true that sixty or seventy years ago copyholds possessed certain advantages. The estate of the copyholder was not liable to his debts either during his life or after his death, for the technical reason—even then obsolete—that the lord was not to have a tenant forced upon him against his will by means of an execution. On the recommendation of the Real Property Commissioners, this unjust advantage was taken away by Acts[2] of 1833 and 1838[3]. The surrenders and admissions of copyholds, again, being recorded on the Court Rolls of the Manor, the security of copyhold titles has never been endangered by liability to the fraudulent suppression of title-deeds, and the assigning of satisfied terms in copyholds has

---

[1] *Life of Lord-Keeper Guildford*, vol. I. p. 36; quoted by the Select Committee on copyholds, *Parl. Pap.* 1837–8, XXIII. 191.

[2] 3 & 4 Will. IV. c. 104 ; 1 & 2 Vict. c. 110, s. 11.

[3] *Third Report*, p. 339.

never been necessary. This advantage of copyholds over freeholds, however, has never weighed much with the legislators who throughout the nineteenth century have fancied themselves on the brink of freehold registration.

The inconveniences of copyhold tenure, on the other hand, were many and serious enough at the beginning of the Queen's reign. In almost all manors a fine had to be paid to the lord on every change of tenancy whether by death or alienation. In manors in which the fine had anciently been arbitrary, it was calculated as a tax on the improved value of the copyholder's land. Such a fine, besides checking alienation, directly discouraged agricultural improvement and the erection of buildings. Copyhold land was found in 1832, in 1838 and in 1851 to be in a most backward agricultural condition, and devoid of drainage improvements and of all buildings but the poorest huts[1].

The heriots, again, which were seizable on the death of a copyholder, caused much annoyance and litigation. There was something peculiarly exasperating about heriots. The Select Committee of 1838 described them as "the most grievous and unjust disadvantage of copyholds[2]." Heriots led not only to strife and ill-will between neighbours, but to constant fraud and evasion. When a yeoman was supposed to be *in extremis*, his family would sell his cattle at a sacrifice or drive them out of the manor, rather than

---

[1] *Third Report, Real Prop. Comm.* p. 334; *Parl. Pap.* 1837-8, xxiii. 191; *ibid.* 1851, xiii. qq. 978-82, 989-92, 1186-92.

[2] *Parl. Pap.* 1837-8, xxiii. 191.

suffer heriot[1]. A more elaborate method of attaining
the same object was to vest the legal estate of the
copyhold in some person domiciled in Scotland as
trustee for the actual copyholder[2]. There was, indeed,
something so extremely "odious and objectionable"
about heriots that respectable gentlemen would not
buy heriotable property; an ex-Lord Mayor who did
so, died in possession of some fine silver plate which
had been presented to him in recognition of his public
services; the plate was seized as heriot[3]. Another
provoking feature of heriots was that they were
capable of almost indefinite multiplication. Whenever
several persons were admitted as tenants on the Court
Rolls, the heriot was multiplied; when copyhold property was sold in parcels, the heriot was multiplied.
If a piece of land were divided up for building purposes,
a hundred heriots might become payable where before
only one heriot was due; "nor were these hydras
susceptible of diminution by any subsequent reunion
of the property[4]."

By the nature of copyhold tenure, independently of
custom, some of the most valuable products of the soil
were distributed between the lord and the copyholder
in such a way as to be of little utility to either. Thus
the lord could not cut the timber growing on the land
without the consent of the tenant, nor could the tenant
cut it, even though he had planted it himself, without
licence from the lord. A similar rule applied to the

[1] *Third Report, Real Prop. Comm.* p. 339.
[2] James Humphreys, *Real Property*, p. 146.
[3] *Parl. Pap.* 1851, xiii. qq. 1346 et seqq.
[4] James Humphreys, *Real Property*, p. 146.

opening of mines. It was not surprising, under these circumstances, that mines remained unworked, and that young trees were banished from copyhold land, the common proverb being that " the oak scorned to grow except on free land[1]." Copyhold land, again, was intermingled with freehold all over the country in a most involved and capricious manner, and it often cost much trouble to identify copyholds. Copyholds were rarely distinguishable by the description of them contained in the Court Rolls, that description being of great antiquity, seldom changed, and often bearing in names and even in quantity no resemblance to any modern description of the parcels. When freeholds and copyholds had been long held by the same owner, the boundaries between the two species of land were often obliterated, and it was in such cases necessary to make, at great expense, both a freehold and a copyhold conveyance of the same land; and even then the purchaser might take an insuperable objection that the vendor could not point out with certainty what part of the estate was freehold and what was copyhold[2]. And if a copyholder, mistaking his tenure, opened a mine or cut timber upon the part of his land which he erroneously believed to be freehold, the land was forfeited to the lord, who might seize it on proving it to be copyhold. On the death intestate of an owner of both freeholds and copyholds, a most impossible situation often arose in manors in which copyholds descended differently from freeholds. Agricultural improvement,

---

[1] *Parl. Pap.* 1837–8, xxiii. 191 et seqq.; *Third Report, Real Prop. Comm.* p. 335.

[2] *Third Report, Real Prop. Comm.* p. 337.

again, was seriously checked by the rule existing in most manors that a copyholder could not grant a lease of his land without a licence from the lord. Even if the lord was willing to grant a licence on reasonable terms, it often happened that he himself had only a partial estate in the manor, and the licence determined with his interest.

All these evils were aggravated by the multiplicity and uncertainty of customs in different manors. Each manor had unto itself a system of law to be sought in oral tradition or in the Court Rolls, kept often by ignorant and negligent stewards[1]. In some manors, to give one example, the widow had one-third of her husband's land for her dower or freebench, in others one-half, in others the whole; sometimes she held it absolutely for her life, sometimes while she remained sole, sometimes only while she remained sole and chaste; the forfeiture being sometimes absolute and sometimes redeemable.

The only material benefits, in brief, which the lord derived from his copyholders, were his fine and his heriot. These benefits bore no proportion to the injury they occasioned to the tenant; and the community at large lost heavily in the impediments which they presented to the improvement and to the free circulation of the land. The Real Property Commissioners arrived at a sound general proposition when they reflected that " wherever there is a subdivision of the right to the profits of the same land between different individuals, although the parts are necessarily equal

---

[1] *Third Report, Real Prop. Comm.* pp. 334, 336.

to the whole in legal interest, they are by no means
so in actual value[1]."

The Commissioners recommended the abolition of
copyhold tenure, proposing that a preliminary measure
should be passed to give increased facilities for the
voluntary enfranchisement of copyholds, and after some
years, a compulsory statute should enfranchise all copyholds. The proposal was strongly resisted by many
sections of the public; by stewards of manors, who
feared that their right to compensation might be
questioned; by powerful lords of manors, possessing
rights over property of great prospective value; by
leading politicians on the ground that an enfranchisement bill would greatly extend the county franchise.
An enfranchisement bill introduced in 1838 was submitted to a Select Committee, which reported that
they "were satisfied that copyhold tenure was a blot
on the juridical system of the country; that the
peculiarities of copyholds were at once highly inconvenient to the owners of the land, and prejudicial to
the general interests of the State; that so long as
copyholds existed, two distinct species of tenure would
prevail, mixed up very generally with each other, and
causing much needless expense and difficulty both in
the investigation of title and in the enjoyment and
alienation of Real Property[2]." In spite of this, the bill
was thrown out, and similar bills of 1839 and 1840
met the same fate. In 1841[3] a mildly permissive

[1] *Third Report*, p. 339.

[2] *Parl. Pap.* 1837–8, xxiii. 191 et seqq.

[3] 4 & 5 Vict. c. 35, amended in 1843 (6 & 7 Vict. c. 23) and in
18 44 (7 & 8 Vict. c. 55).

measure was at last carried, affording certain facilities
for the enfranchisement of copyholds in cases where
the lord or the tenant was not entitled to the whole
estate in the manor or the land. It provided that
if both lord and tenant agreed, copyholds might be
enfranchised in consideration of an annual rent-charge,
or of the conveyance of other lands, or of money paid
by the tenant to the lord, and provision was made for
charging the enfranchised land with money so paid,
by way of mortgage. The same Act provided that
fines, heriots, rents, reliefs, etc., and the lord's interest
in timber and mines, might be commuted by agreement into a rent varying or not (as agreed) with the
price of corn, together with a small fixed fine on
death or alienation[1]. Provision was also made for the
commutation of the lord's rights throughout entire
manors, with the consent of the Copyhold Commissioners established by the Act. The same Act abolished
some of the more tedious and vexatious formalities
attending the transfer of copyholds, by enacting that
lords or stewards out of the manor might make grants
of copyholds[2], that presentments of surrenders made
out of court should be unnecessary[3], that admittance
might be had out of the manor, without holding a
court, and without presentment of the preceding
surrender[4], that a devisee should be admitted without
a presentment of the will, by merely delivering a copy
of the will to the steward[5]. It had been found, too,
that in manors where there were but few copyholders,

[1] 4 & 5 Vict. c. 35, s. 14.
[2] s. 87 of Act.   [3] s. 89 of Act.   [4] s. 88 of Act.
[5] s. 90 of Act.

lords were unwilling to grant enfranchisement, from an apprehension that they might be unable to muster sufficient for holding a court[1]; the Act therefore provided that customary courts might be held without the presence of any copyholder[2], except when by the custom of the manor the lord was authorized to grant common or waste land with the consent of the homage.

The Act of 1841 formed a starting-point of reform, but was a failure in practice. It produced very little enfranchisement and very little commutation, and it soon became evident that compulsory powers would have to be conferred on copyhold tenants. Attempts to do so were at first unsuccessful; but in 1851 a Select Committee took an enormous amount of evidence on the evils of copyhold tenure and the failure of the Act of 1841; and in the following year Lord Brougham procured the passing of an Act[3] which, in conjunction with an Act of 1858, made enfranchisement compulsory at the instance of either lord or tenant. Under these Acts, if enfranchisement took place at the instance of the tenant, the compensation was to be a gross sum of money; if at the instance of the lord, an annual rent-charge issuing out of the enfranchised land; but other forms of compensation might be agreed on with the sanction of the Copyhold Commissioners[4], and if the parties could not agree on the amount of compensation the same Commissioners might award reasonable com-

[1] *Third Report, Real Prop. Comm.* p. 340.

[2] s. 86 of Act.

[3] Copyhold Acts of 1852 and 1858.   15 & 16 Vict. c. 51 ; 21 & 22 Vict. c. 94.

[4] 15 & 16 Vict. c. 51, s. 7 ; 21 & 22 Vict. c. 94, s. 21.

pensation.   Enfranchisements under the Acts were
held to be valid irrespectively of the validity of the
lord's title; a great difficulty was thus removed which
had formerly arisen from the necessity of investigating
the lord's title when an enfranchisement was contemplated[1].

The Copyhold Acts of 1852 and 1858 were more
successful than preceding Acts; extensive enfranchisements were effected under them.   There can be no
doubt that they gave an increased market-value to
the lord's rights, by enabling him to convert the
varying and uncertain income from fines and heriots
into a fixed yearly rent-charge ; and they increased the
market-value of the copyholder's interest, by enabling
him to compel enfranchisement on moderate terms
and on a fixed principle of calculation known to everyone[2].

More recent Acts have made sundry improvements
in the machinery of enfranchisement.   The Copyhold
Act of 1887 prevented enclosures of waste and common
lands from taking place without regard to the interests
of the public or of the labouring population.   There
was in some manors a custom for the lord with the
consent of the homage to grant land out of the waste
lands of the manor to be held by copyhold tenure.
The homage might consist of copyholders nominated
by the steward in the interest of the lord, and in this
way it often happened that parts of rural commons
vanished from the public view without even the cogni-

---

[1] *Kerr* v. *Pawson*, Rolls, 4 Jur. Rep. N.S. 425.

[2] Cuddon on *Copyholds* (1859), pp. 5 et seqq.

zance of the persons having rights over them[1].   The
Act of 1887 therefore provided that no such grant of
common or waste land should in future be valid without
the consent of the Land Commissioners (now of the
Board of Agriculture).   The Act[2] also closed the only
remaining source for the creation of new copyholds by
declaring that land so granted out of the waste or
common should be freehold and not copyhold.   The
same Act entitled surrenderees to be admitted by
attorney, a privilege on which they could not previously
insist; and provided that on a statutory enfranchisement the land should escheat to the lord of the manor
and not, as formerly, to the lord of whom he held.
The Copyhold Act of 1894, lastly, contains certain new
regulations for enfranchisements to be awarded by the
Board of Agriculture[3]; and provides for the extinction,
at the instance of either lord or tenant, of any manorial
incident whatsoever affecting any land whether freehold
or copyhold.

It remains to give a short account of another tenure
which, although excluded from the honours of realty, is
of the utmost economic importance in England.   Leaseholds, being more than other tenures of a contractual
nature, might reasonably be expected to be less marred
with superfluous technicalities.   This to a certain
extent is the case.   The judges of our law-courts have
nevertheless contrived to introduce sundry refinements
distinguished more for elegance than for policy or
common sense.   It is worth observing with regard to

---

[1] Shaw Lefevre, *Agrarian Tenures*, p. 64.

[2] 52 & 53 Vict. c. 30.

[3] 57 & 58 Vict. c. 46, ss. 2, 5–8, 94.

many of the antique rules of law which have received such scant respect from modern legislation, that the logical coherence of a rule with other rules is no guarantee of the justice or the expediency of that rule. If a number of excellent persons are furnished with a number of excellent elementary propositions of law, and if to those persons be entrusted the task of making rules to meet all the exigencies of human life solely by the permutation, combination and elaboration of those propositions, then the resulting rules may be either good, indifferent, unworkable, or positively mischievous; if they are expedient and just, they are so by the merest chance.

The rent paid by a leaseholder, for example, was regarded by our judges as only a constituent part of the landlord's total right in the land; his total right or reversion they regarded as one and indivisible. Therefore, if the reversion was accidentally destroyed by merger in a larger estate, the curious but unpleasant consequence arose that the landlord lost his rent. This curiosity of the law was removed by the Transfer of Property Act, 1844, and the Real Property Act of 1845[1], which provided that on the destruction of a reversion by surrender or merger, the next vested estate in the land should be deemed the reversion for the purpose of preserving the rent and other incidents of the lease[2]. But not only the reversion was considered entire and indivisible;—if the landlord stipulated for a right of re-entry on breach of the covenants of

[1] 7 & 8 Vict. c. 76 ; 8 & 9 Vict. c. 106.

[2] The inconvenience had already been removed with regard to leases surrendered in order to be renewed by St. 4 Geo. II. c. 28, s. 6.

the lease, this right also was considered entire and indivisible. It followed that if the landlord sold *part* of the leased land, the right of re-entry was destroyed entirely, and could not be exercised either by the purchaser or by the landlord. It followed also, or it was conceived to follow, that if the landlord licensed the tenant to do an act which was a breach of any covenant, or which was not to be done without licence, the right of re-entry attaching to that particular act was for ever destroyed. The same thing happened if the landlord expressly waived his right of re-entry on a breach of a covenant. The natural result was that landlords dared not allow breaches of covenants, however desirable such breaches might become to both parties by change of circumstances. These absurdities and many others like them were swept away, mostly on the suggestion of Joshua Williams, by " Lord St Leonards' Act " of 1859 and " Lord Cranworth's Act " of 1860[1], extended by the Conveyancing Act of 1881[2].

In recent times leasehold tenure has come to some extent within the scope of the great agitation known as the Land Question. We have seen that the Land Question of England has been primarily a question as to the fate of the agricultural labourer. But the position of the tenant-farmer has also been found to be in many respects in need of reform. His position has in many respects been found to be such as not to yield the best results either in his own or the public interest. The freetrader of the earlier half of the century would

[1] 22 & 23 Vict. c. 35, ss. 1–3 ; 23 & 24 Vict. c. 38, s. 6 ; 44 & 45 Vict. c. 41, ss. 10, 12.

[2] *Vide Parl. Pap.* 1857, vol. xviii. Appendix, pp. 307 et seqq.

have dismissed the matter by saying: " let the sane
adult tenant make his own terms with the landowner,
like other sane adults; he is the best judge of his own
interests; perfect freedom of contract between the
landlord and the tenant will yield the best results not
only for the contracting parties, but also for the community at large." During the latter half of the century
the practical application of the *laisser faire* doctrine
has been considerably qualified, and its sphere of
operation considerably narrowed. Analysis has shown
that freedom of contract exists only when the contracting parties are, roughly and approximately, on an
equal footing for the purposes of their bargain. The
tenant would have freedom of contract if he had the
means of transporting himself and his stock and fixtures
elsewhere, if he had sufficient intelligence and information always to know his best market, and if neither
indolence nor dread of change, nor love of home,
friends and country intervened to keep him from that
market.

The landowner is in possession of an article strictly
limited in quantity, and the English land-law has so
operated as to place this scarce article in the hands
of a relatively small number of persons. It is true
that public opinion restrains owners of agricultural
land from taking the full advantage of their privileges.
" In England," says the late Francis Walker, " the
sentiment is universal that there are classes who by
reason of wealth, education and social position are
bound to do and to forbear much out of regard to
the interests of classes deemed to be permanently and
hopelessly weak." In England, if a gentleman should

undertake to force up his rents, instead of gaining
increase of style and state through an enlargement of
his rent-roll thus obtained, he would find his social
standing destroyed; and it has accordingly been a
fact, until a quarter of a century ago, that the rent
of agricultural land has seldom been the maximum
value of the occupancy[1]. But the great agricultural
depression which began in 1880, and the increase
of American competition, have greatly changed the
tenant-farmer's position for the worse. It is said,
again, that landlords do not usually take advantage
of their right to give six months' notice to quit. But
in those very cases in which a restraining agency is
most wanted—for example, when a mortgagee is in
possession—public opinion is powerless; and at the
best, public opinion cannot give the tenant that without
which he can never safely invest capital in the soil,
namely, security of tenure and of compensation for
improvements. The same reasons, in short, which led
to the Land Acts of Ireland, have in England led to
some legislative measures interfering with the freedom
of contract beween landlord and tenant, or rather, with
the freedom of contract of the landlord. In the interests of the tenant as well as of the public at large,
the hands of the weaker party have been strengthened.

Before the wars of the French Revolution agricultural leases for terms of years were the rule rather than
the exception in England. Throughout the Queen's
reign tenancies from year to year have prevailed almost universally. The change, according to Mr Shaw

---

[1] *Political Economy*, Part IV. ch. II.

Lefevre[1], was caused by the great fluctuations in prices of agricultural produce during those wars, which indisposed both landlords and tenants to tie their hands by long leases; the practice was strengthened after the Reform Act of 1832 by the political influence which landowners acquired in proportion to the number of their voting tenants holding precariously from year to year.

At the commencement of the Queen's reign, the yearly tenant was dismissable by a six months' notice, and had in general no right to claim compensation for unexhausted improvements. This caused much dissatisfaction among the farming classes, especially when foreign competition began to be keenly felt in agricultural production. Tenants complained that they had no security for the capital which they invested in the soil; the public at large complained that this insecurity prevented the tenant from investing as large an amount for agricultural purposes as he otherwise would, and that the producing power of the country was thus not brought up to its full pitch. Experience showed that in the absence of a right to claim compensation, the tenant would spend no more on the improvement of the land, especially towards the end of his term of tenancy, than was just barely sufficient to maintain his average rate of production and to keep within the covenants of the lease against exhaustion of the soil[2]. It was also complained that the half-year's notice to quit increased the tenant's insecurity, deterred him from investing much capital in the soil, and dis-

[1] *Agrarian Tenures*, p. 49.
[2] *Vide* Duke of Richmond in 1875, Hansard, ccxxii. p. 1683.

couraged him from so rotating his crops as to obtain the greatest possible production.

The Law of Distress, again, was all in favour of the landlord. By this remedy he could obtain arrears of rent in priority to other creditors of the tenant-farmer, and seize all stock on the land even though it were known to belong to persons other than the tenant. The great length of the period of distress—six years— enabled the landlord to keep his right in reserve until the stock or goods of others chanced to be on the tenant's farm. It was complained that this relic of feudalism placed the tenant at the landlord's mercy; that it impaired the general credit of the tenant and rendered it impossible for him to obtain agricultural machinery or breeding stock on hire; that it gave the landlord an unfair preference over other creditors. It was contended that there was no difference in the commercial position of the landlord who supplied the land, and the man who supplied any other commodity; and that the right of distress should be altogether abolished[1]. In favour of the retention of the right of distress, on the other hand, it was urged that it gave additional security to mortgagees, and in certain cases to small annuitants; that if it were abolished, some more injurious substitute would have to be introduced, such as the payment of rent in advance, the finding of security, bills of sale, or stringent powers of immediate re-entry; that it was a cheap and easy remedy, which,

[1] Report of Royal Commission on Agricultural Interests, *Parl. Pap.* 1882, vol. xiv. pp. 33 et seqq.; Report of Select Committee on Law of Distress, *Parl. Pap.* 1882, vol. viii. pp. 273 et seqq.

though rarely enforced, was of great practical use; that from the peculiarity of his position, and from the fact of his claim continually accruing, the landlord justly had a preferential right over the ordinary creditor[1].

Fixtures formed another point on which the law cherished the landowner. The Common Law maxim "quicquid plantatur solo, solo cedit" was applied in all strictness to agricultural fixtures; the Courts decided in the beginning of the nineteenth century that agricultural fixtures of all kinds became the absolute property of the landlord, and could not be removed by the tenant even during his term, and even although no damage might be done by the removal[2].

All these complaints and inconveniences, set forth in 1875 in a report of the Chambers of Agriculture, led in the same year to the introduction of the first Agricultural Holdings Bill. The bill dealt with compensation for improvements, with the law of fixtures, and with the length of notices to quit. On all these points the bill proposed to improve the tenant's position, but only *in the absence* of any contrary agreement between the landlord and the tenant. The bill was keenly contested. Some objected to it on the ground that it interfered, or might pave the way to an interference, with Freedom of Contract, and on the more general ground that "restrictive legislation for the attainment of purely economic ends had in the

---

[1] *Parl. Pap.* 1882, vol. VIII. pp. 269 et seqq.

[2] 1803; *Elwes* v. *Mawe*, 3 East, K. B. 38. An Act of 1851 (14 & 15 Vict. c. 25) permitted an agricultural tenant to remove farm buildings, engines, and machinery erected by him *with* the consent of the landlord, unless the latter should elect to purchase them.

past been found unnecessary and injurious[1]." Others
denied that there was any real freedom of contract
between tenant and landlord, and asserted that the
tenant was practically compelled to accept the terms
offered by the landlord; but they objected to the bill
on the ground that it allowed landlords to contract
themselves out of its provisions; they would like to
see the measure made compulsory[2].

The bill, after some small amendments, became
the Agricultural Holdings Act of 1875[3]. It remained
largely a dead letter, the greater number of landlords
immediately excluding its operation[4]. The following
years were marked by an unprecedented succession
of bad harvests and by a great pressure of foreign
competition. Many tenants were in arrear with their
rent, and landlords resorted freely to their right of
distress[5]. In 1879 a Royal Commission was appointed
" to inquire into the depressed condition of the agricultural interest and the causes to which it was owing."
After an exhaustive inquiry the Commission reported
in 1882, recommending that further legislative provision
should be made for securing to tenants the compensation to which they were equitably entitled in respect
of their outlay, and that the principles of the Agricultural Holdings Act of 1875 relating to compensation
should be made compulsory in all cases where such
compensation was not otherwise provided for[6]. With
regard to the Law of Distress, they recommended that

[1] Duke of Argyll, Hansard, ccxxiii. p. 949.

[2] Hansard, ccxxv. pp. 461, 464, 1708.

[3] 38 & 39 Vict. c. 92.   [4] *Parl. Pap.* 1882, vol. xiv. p. 31.

[5] *Ibid.* 1882, vol. xiv. p. 22.   [6] *Ibid.* pp. 31 et seqq.

the power of distraint should be limited to two years, and that hired machinery and agisted cattle should be exempted from the operation of the law[1].

These and other recommendations of the Commission were carried out in the Agricultural Holdings Act of 1883[2]; and on this occasion hardly a word was heard in Parliament about non-interference with the freedom of contract imagined to exist between the landlord and the tenant. The Act, without prejudicing claims for compensation existing under local customs, provides that every tenant making any of the improvements specified shall be entitled on the determination of his tenancy to obtain from the landlord such sum as fairly represents the value of the improvement to an incoming tenant. Improvements are divided by the Act into three classes. For the execution of "permanent" improvements, such as buildings, fences, etc., the landlord's written consent must be obtained, otherwise the right to compensation will not arise. For "temporary" improvements neither the consent of the landlord nor notice to him is required; "Drainage" improvements form a class by themselves, due to their agricultural importance and to the fact that till lately they have been strangely neglected in England[3]. We have seen that in our rural economy it is the landlord and not the tenant, who executes drainage improvements. The Act enables the tenant to put pressure on the landlord; if the landlord will not drain, the

[1] *Parl. Pap.* 1882, vol. XIV. p. 33.

[2] 46 & 47 Vict. c. 61, amended by 50 & 51 Vict. c. 26; 53 & 54 Vict. c. 57; and 58 & 59 Vict. c. 27.

[3] *Vide supra*, p. 99.

tenant may do so, and may charge the landlord with
compensation on the determination of his tenancy.
The exact amount and the time and mode of payment
of the "fair and reasonable" compensation of the Act
are allowed to be defined by agreement in the lease, or
by subsequent agreement, or by arbitration; but the
tenant's right to compensation under the Act is indefeasible, and any agreement by which he deprives
himself of the right is void both at law and in equity[1].
The Act also repeats, but still in a merely permissive
form, a provision of the Act of 1875 substituting
a year's notice to quit for half-a-year's notice in a
tenancy from year to year. With regard to the law of
fixtures, the Act provides that engines, machinery,
fencing and buildings erected by the tenant shall
become the absolute property of the tenant and re-
movable by him, the landlord however having an
option of purchase. The Law of Distress, lastly, has
been amended by the Act, and its hardships considerably mitigated. The six years of rent recoverable by
distress are reduced to one year; the time within which
a distress may be redeemed is extended from five to
fifteen days; agricultural machinery and agisted cattle
are exempted from distress; and all distresses are
required to be taken by certificated bailiffs. By the
Law of Distress Amendment Act of 1888[2] these provisions are extended to all tenancies; and the bedding,
clothes, and tools of trade of a tenant up to the value
of £5 are exempted from distress.

In two or three other instances has the legislature

[1] s. 55 of Act.   [2] 51 & 52 Vict. c. 21.

recently intervened to strengthen the tenant in his negotiations with the landlord.

The Ground Game Act of 1880[1] provides that every tenant shall have a right, indefeasible and inseparable from his occupation, to kill ground game on land in his occupation concurrently with any other person entitled to kill the same; and that all agreements in contravention of this right shall be void. The Act removed a "long felt grievance." Previously to the Act, hardly a single landlord was willing to grant his tenants the right of destroying the ground game which ravaged their crops. So strong were sporting notions and traditions that nothing less than an Act of Parliament could remedy the evil. In the debates on the measure it was admitted by all that the destruction of crops by game, often aggravated by overpreservation, was a real misfortune. It was also generally recognized that the tenant could no longer be left helpless against these mischievous animals. The only difficulty was as to the method. Some proposed that the tenant should be compensated in money; others, that hares and rabbits should be taken out of the category of game and degraded to the condition of rats[2]. Sir William Harcourt proposed to interfere with Freedom of Contract by giving the tenant an indefeasible right of killing ground game on his farm. "It appeared to him a sound principle that when one placed a man in occupation of the soil, one should not impose upon him conditions that practically made his occupation idle[3]." The last proposal was adopted, notwithstanding some

[1] 43 & 44 Vict. c. 47.   [2] Hansard, CCLIV. pp. 1732, 1746.
[3] *Ibid.* CCLII. p. 597.

faint resistance on the score of the freedom of contract[1].
The Act has in practice most successfully attained its
object. In many districts hares have almost totally
disappeared; indeed it has become necessary to in-
stitute a close time for the sale of hares[2].

The tenant has been aided by legislation, again, in
connection with conditions of re-entry on breach of
covenants other than covenants to pay money. Tenants
of valuable farms and other property who had by mere
oversight committed breaches of covenants, had suffered
much hardship through the rigorous exercise of the
right of re-entry. To prevent this, the Conveyancing
Act of 1881[3] has made conditions of re-entry unenforce-
able until the tenant has had notice of the breach of
covenant and a reasonable time to remedy the breach
or make compensation; and even after the lapse of
this "reasonable time" the Court may grant relief on
such terms as it thinks fit, at any time before the
landlord has actually recovered possession of the
premises.

Parliament has again interfered with the freedom
of contract of the landlord by the Tithe Act of 1891[4].
Before that date it had been the almost universal
practice for landowners to arrange in their agreements
with their tenants that tithe rent-charge should be
paid by the latter. In periods of agricultural depression this arrangement had pressed severely on
tenants, especially as tithe receivers were not generally
willing to make abatements on account of hard times.

[1] Hansard, CCLII. pp. 1725, 1743; CCLIV. pp. 1688, 1713.
[2] St. 55 & 56 Vict. c. 8; Lefevre, *Agrarian Tenures*, p. 54.
[3] 44 & 45 Vict. c. 41, s. 14.   [4] 54 & 55 Vict. c. 8.

Much complaint consequently arose, and in Wales,
where a large majority of tenants paying tithe rent-
charge were Nonconformists, scenes of violence took
place and some tenants absolutely refused to pay[1].
The Tithe Act of 1891 now provides that tithe rent-
charge shall be payable by the landowner, and that any
contract made between him and the tenant or occupier,
for the payment of tithe rent-charge by the latter,
shall be void.

Before leaving this subject it may be worth while
just to mention a recent attempt to facilitate the
conversion of agricultural tenancies into ownerships.
By a provision[2] of the Small Agricultural Holdings Act
of 1892 County Councils are empowered to advance
public money to tenants of lands of 50 acres and under,
or of £50 annual value and under, to the extent of
four-fifths of the purchase money, to enable them to
purchase their holdings from their landlords.   Another
project, known as leasehold enfranchisement, has for
some time been before the public.   Its promoters
propose to entitle urban leaseholders, holding under a
lease of twenty years unexpired, to purchase the freehold of their houses for a reasonable price, or, at their
option, for a perpetual rent-charge.   The project has
more than once been considered by Parliament.   Since,
however, it has had no legislative results, it need not
occupy us any further[3].

[1] *Vide* Sir M. Hicks-Beach in Hansard, cccLxix. p. 241.

[2] s. 17.

[3] Much information on the subject is to be found in the Report of
the Royal Commission on the Housing of the Working Classes, *Parl.
Pap.* 1885, vols. xxx. and xxxi.; and in that of the Town Holdings
Committee, *Parl. Pap.* 1887, vol. xiii. pp. 41 et seqq.; and *Parl. Pap.*
1888, vol. xxii.

CHAPTER IV.

TESTAMENTS AND INTESTACY.

In the year 1837 the testamentary law of England had gradually degenerated into a condition of defectiveness and bewildering chaos with which the Courts of law and equity were unable to cope, and a comprehensive statutory remedy was urgently needed. We shall begin by describing the modes in which wills were then executed.

It is obvious that wills are always more than other legal documents open to the dangers of fraud, perjury and forgery, duress and undue influence, and to doubts as to the mental capacity of the testator, for the reason that the testator is necessarily unable personally to guard against these dangers at the time when the will takes effect. On this account most or all systems of law have required some formality or other to be observed in the execution of wills. The expediency of requiring a formality obviously applies to wills of every description of property; if any difference be made in the stringency of the requirement, it should depend on the value rather than on the nature of the property. In England, however, there were in 1837 no less than six methods of executing wills, according to the nature of the property bequeathed. Wills of freeholds were nominally required to be in writing signed by the testator in the presence of three credible witnesses; but it was held by the Courts that the name of the testator appearing in any part of the will was a sufficient signature; this naturally gave an opening for fraud, and led to a difficult distinction between "perfect" and "imperfect" wills. The witnesses, again, were not required to be present together at the same time, and they were held to subscribe in the testator's presence if he might *possibly* see them, as through a broken window, or from a carriage in the street through a window into an office[1]. Wills of leaseholds and personalty might be by simple parol if the property was worth less than £30; if more than £30, by parol with certain superadded requirements of the Statute of Frauds; but the power of making nuncupative wills was seldom exercised. If wills of personalty were in writing, they might be made in any form, without signature or witnesses; a scrap of paper, a memorandum in ink or pencil was enough, though not seen by or read to the testator[2]. Wills of estates *pur autre vie* were required at law to be made like wills of fee-simple estates, but in equity a will without witnesses was valid, unless the heir were special occupant. Wills of money in the Funds were required by statute to be in writing attested by two

[1] *Fourth Report, Real Prop. Comm.* p. 16; Tyrrell, *Evidence,* ch. VIII. § 5.

[2] *Fourth Report, Real Prop. Comm.* p. 7.

credible witnesses, but in equity witnesses were unnecessary[1]. Wills of copyholds were made in writing
or by parol or in other ways according to the customs
of manors. Wills made in exercise of powers of appointment might be required to be executed with or
without any number of witnesses or with any other
solemnity at the caprice of the donor of the power.
" Every combination of the solemnities required by law,
and several solemnities not required by any law, were
occasionally presented by powers of appointment[2]."

This variety of rules for a similar purpose naturally
occasioned much litigation on questions of mere form,
and caused innumerable mistakes which defeated the
intentions of testators and the expectations of their
friends. Disappointments most frequently occurred in
the case of money directed to be laid out in the
purchase of land, which would only pass by a will
executed like a will of fee-simple estates. The public,
also, had never learnt to understand the distinction
by which freehold land required three witnesses, and
leasehold no witnesses at all[3].

Much mischief was also done by the rule of law
which regarded a will as a present or immediate
conveyance. While after-acquired personalty could be
validly bequeathed, no will could affect after-acquired
freeholds; and even with regard to freeholds in the
possession of the testator at the time of making the
will, a devise could not take effect unless the estate
to which the testator was entitled when he made the

---

[1] *Bank of England* v. *Moffat*, 3 Bro. C. C. 260.

[2] *Fourth Report, Real Prop. Comm.* p. 12.

[3] *Ibid.* pp. 13, 58.

will continued unaltered till his death. This principle, accounted for by several ingenious theories, was pushed to such a length that a feoffment made by a testator to his own use, or with a resulting use, or made expressly to give effect to his will, would render his will *pro tanto* void. It was even held that a devise might become void by a merely *intended* alteration of the testator's estate, by any deed or contract not effectual as a conveyance; for example, by a contract for the sale of land subsequently rescinded[1]. A mortgage and reconveyance was an implied revocation in law but not in equity; an exchange was an implied revocation in law, but a partition was not. These refinements made it necessary for a testator to republish his will or make a codicil, whenever he acquired new property. The same principle caused every residuary devise to comprise only such land as had not before been expressed to be given; therefore any property that lapsed went to the heir, contrary to the obvious intention of the testator.

An even more erratic part of the testamentary law was that which dealt with the interpretation of wills. A will was indeed considered to be the disposition of a person *inops consilii,* and judges took cognizance of the disposition of testators to make their wills in secrecy, and to delay the making until the last moment. They also professed the greatest anxiety to give effect to every proper intention which could be collected from the terms used in wills. But they found it absolutely essential to establish for themselves fixed

[1] *Fourth Report, Real Prop. Comm.* pp. 24, 28.

rules of construction. If wills, they said, were to be construed according to the unfettered discretion of judges without reference to any fixed rules of interpretation, no reliance could be placed on any title arising under a will until its construction should have been decided in Court, and every will upon which the slightest doubt could be raised must become the subject of litigation. If the Courts were to exercise an unlimited latitude of forming conjectures respecting the intentions of testators, the conjectures of an advising counsel might differ from the opinion of a judge[1]. "It was therefore necessary to establish rules of construction, and important to uphold them, that all who might have to advise might be able to give opinions on titles with safety[2]."

It appears, then, that rules of construction were (and are) a necessary evil. The great vice of the English rules of construction was that they were entirely out of harmony with the common sense of laymen. Common forms of expression used by ordinary men in an ordinary sense, were interpreted by the Courts in a totally different sense. Indeed, our judges were conscious of the absurdity of the rules which they were bound to apply. In the case of *Briscoe* v. *Clark*, Lord Chief Justice Mansfield remarked, "I have no doubt that our decision will be contrary to the real intention of the testator[3]." In *Jesson* v. *Wright*, Lord Eldon observed, "According to the words of the will it is absurd to suppose that the testator could have

---

[1] John Tyrrell, *Evidence*, ch. XII.

[2] Lord Redesdale in *Jesson* v. *Wright* (2 Bligh P. C. 56).

[3] Doe d. *Briscoe* v. *Clark* (2 Bosanquet and Puller, 348).

such intentions as the rules of law compel us to ascribe to his will[1]." So again Lord Mansfield, speaking of the rule that an unlimited devise gives only an estate for life: "I verily believe that in almost every case where by law a general devise of land is reduced to an estate for life, the intention of the testator is thwarted[2]." So Lord Chief Justice Wilmot, referring to the rule that "dying without issue" means a general failure of issue: "It is a repeal of that great law of all language, the grammar, and it confounds present and future time together. It is the most intolerable tyranny, the grossest injustice, to say that the words ('dying without issue') mark one idea, when the man who uses them and all who read and hear them are convinced they mark another[3]." So strongly did judges feel the injustice of such rules, that they endeavoured to evade them by creating all sorts of exceptions whenever possible. To the rule of "dying without issue," for example, there were no less than six established classes of exceptions[4]. Judges gradually came to consider not what the real intention of the testator was, but whether there was any additional manifestation of intention sufficient to allow them to bring the case before them within an exception; and the difficulty of distinguishing the cases within the exception from the cases within the rule created more uncertainty than the obscurity of the meaning of the testator.

The evil effect of irrational rules of construction in

[1] 2 Bligh P. C. 50.

[2] In Right d. *Mitchell* v. *Sidebotham* (Douglas, Rep. 763).

[3] In *Keiley* v. *Fowler* (Wilm. Rep. 408).

[4] Jarman on *Wills*, 564.

increasing litigation was already felt in the seventeenth
century. Sir Matthew Hale estimated that since the
Statute of Wills "more questions had arisen touching
the construction of wills than in any five general titles
of the law besides[1]." Lord Kenyon declared that "few
questions arose on the construction of deeds when
compared with those which daily arose on wills[2]."
And John Tyrrell deposed before the Real Property
Commission that nearly half the litigation relating to
Real Property was occasioned by the rules of construction of wills[3].

The Real Property Commissioners proposed a radical
measure of reform; and their detailed recommendations
were carried out almost literally by the Wills Act of
1837[4]. This important statute has provided a simple
and uniform mode of execution for all wills. It has
remedied the indefiniteness and complexity of wills of
freeholds, the dangerous laxity and informality of wills
of personalty, and the vagaries of powers of appointment by will, and of copyhold wills. In order to
prevent fraud, the testator's signature is required to
be at the foot of the will, and no signature can give
effect to any disposition written underneath it[5]. The
presence of witnesses is required in order to prevent
fraud or coercion, and to prove the capacity of the
testator; the number *two* was fixed on instead of *one*,

---

[1] In his "Treatise concerning Registry"; quoted in *Fourth Report*,
Real Prop. Comm. p. 3.

[2] In Denn d. *Moor* v. *Mellor* (5 Term Rep. 561).

[3] John Tyrrell, *Evidence*, p. 315.

[4] 7 Will. IV. & 4 Vict. c. 26.

[5] s. 9 of the Act, elaborated by St. 15 & 16 Vict. c. 24.

in order to increase the chance that a witness would be living at the death of the testator, and in order to bring into play the difficulty of engaging an accomplice, the necessity of rewarding him, and the danger to be apprehended from his giving information; the two witnesses are required to be present *together*, in order to remove the possibility of getting two accomplices at different times, and in order to force them to tell exactly the same story in Court, and thus to render perjury more easily discoverable by cross-examination[1].

The Act further provides that a will shall be construed to speak as if executed immediately before death; that no subsequent disposition of property shall prevent its operation with respect to the property owned by the testator at his death; and that property comprised in lapsed devises shall go to the general residuary devisee. The Act has abolished the judge-made rules of construction, together with their exceptions, and has substituted new rules, which in the main give to phrases and expressions the meanings which they bear to the ordinary layman. The Real Property Commissioners had considered a proposal that the strict rules of law governing the interpretation of deeds should be extended to wills, but they had come to the conclusion that this would place too much restraint on testamentary disposition. They realized how impossible it is in cases of sudden illness to make wills with the care and consideration which attend the preparation of deeds, how often there is not time to call in professional legal assistance, and how important

---

[1] *Fourth Report, Real Prop. Comm.* pp. 17, 18.

it is that wills should be expressed in such words as to be intelligible to the testator himself and to his family[1]. Other improvements were introduced by the Act, too numerous to mention. The methods of revoking a will were made securer and more definite. The law relating to lapses was amended on those points in which it ran counter to the obvious intention of testators, viz., in devises for an estate tail, and in devises to the testator's own issue. The age for making testaments of personalty was raised to twenty-one years, the Real Property Commissioners having " seen no reason for any exception to the rule of law which for the protection of minors renders them incapable of making any disposition or contract[2]."

All these reforms brought the law of the construction and execution of wills to a reasonable degree of efficiency. Much friction however continued to be caused by another branch of testamentary law, viz., the law of probate and letters of administration. A will of freeholds did not require to be proved unless litigation actually arose, and then it was proved in a Common Law Court like a deed. But a will of personalty had to be proved, whether disputed or not, in one or more of the Courts of Probate. The latter numbered about 380 at the beginning of the Queen's reign, although their exact number could not be ascertained, for the right of holding them was continually being disputed between ecclesiastic superiors and inferiors, and between spiritual and lay parties[3]. The Courts of Probate

---

[1] *Fourth Report*, p. 3 ; Tyrrell's *Evidence*, ch. XII.

[2] *Fourth Report*, p. 23.

[3] *Ibid.* p. 53.

granted probates and letters of administration, and settled testamentary suits. Each Court governed its own procedure and practice. Few of them had secure places for the custody of the important documents which they compelled parties to deposit, and in many of them no pretence even was made of preserving such documents. The extent of their jurisdiction was often obscured by the existence of Royal peculiars, of peculiars of universities and colleges, of impropriate rectories, of Honours and manors, of peculiars of bishops and archbishops. Endless difficulties were caused by the variety and the incompetence of these Courts. An executor had often to take out probate for one will in some half-a-dozen Courts, according as the will comprised leaseholds, specialty debts, judgment debts, simple contract debts, money in the Funds, shares in public companies, or moveable chattels. Sometimes the testator's office or station required his will to be proved in a particular Court; and whenever a testator left property within a peculiar from which no appeal lay to the Archbishop's Court, an additional probate of the will had to be taken out[1]. Much trouble was caused, too, by the rules of "bona notabilia" and the consequent voidness or voidability of wills. But most of all, the transfer of Real Property was delayed by the numerous and conflicting testamentary jurisdictions. We have noticed the practice, prevalent before 1845, of securing purchasers of land by vesting satisfied terms in trustees[2]. When such trustees died, their

---

[1] *Fourth Report, Real Prop. Comm.* pp. 42 et seqq.
[2] *Vide sup.* p. 4.

personal representatives generally omitted to take out probate or letters of administration for the satisfied term, through not knowing of its existence; even if they knew, they often found themselves unable to take out " prerogative probate " of the will, and no other probate was safe for the purpose of assigning the term. This caused " much expense and vexation, and general complaint, calling loudly for a remedy[1]."

The Real Property Commissioners reported that the Spiritual Courts were not adapted for testamentary suits or for any other form of testamentary jurisdiction. They recommended that a single Central Court of Probate should be established, having jurisdiction over the whole of England and Wales, and possessing a central registry for all wills of personalty; and that the contentious jurisdiction of the Ecclesiastical Courts should be transferred to the Court of Chancery[2]. To carry out this recommendation Lord Campbell and Lord Chief Baron Pollock introduced bills in 1835 and in 1837, but without achieving any practical result. Year after year the subject was renewed by Lord Lyndhurst, by Lord Cranworth, and by Lord St Leonards; but it was not till 1857 that the Court of Probate Act[3] became law. This Act abolished the testamentary jurisdiction of the Ecclesiastical Courts and established the Court of Probate in which all wills of personalty were required to be proved.

In the preceding year another Statute[4] had introduced uniformity into the rules governing the intestate

---

[1] *Real Prop. Comm., First Report*, p. 59; *Fourth Report*, p. 54.

[2] *Fourth Report*, pp. 54, 57, and 69.

[3] 20 & 21 Vict. c. 77.			[4] 19 & 20 Vict. c. 94.

distribution of personalty, by abolishing the peculiar and troublesome customs of the City of London, the Province of York, and other places. This Statute, together with the Real Property Inheritance Act of 1833, the Wills Act of 1837, and the Court of Probate Act of 1857, placed the law of testaments and intestacy on a workable footing, and removed most of the defects and anomalies which had been allowed to creep into it by the previous negligence of the legislature.

The remaining legislative measures and projects relating to this part of the law may be more briefly dealt with. Their general tendency has been to extend to real property the rules governing the devolution of personalty. Since the middle of the century efforts have continually been made to establish a "real" or "realty" representative corresponding to the personal representative of a deceased person, and to assimilate the law of descent of realty to that of personalty.

Many difficulties have in the past been caused by the absence of a real representative, and by the rule of law making it unnecessary either to prove a will of realty or to take out letters of administration for real estate. A trustee of real estate, for example, might die intestate, leaving an infant heir, and to get the legal estate out of the infant it would be necessary to go to Chancery at an expense of £30 or £40 at the least; or he might leave as his heir some distant cousin, to ascertain whose pedigree it might be necessary to go back to the reign of Queen Anne or perhaps further, and whose pedigree, when discovered, thenceforth formed a necessary link in the title; or the trustee might make a will raising the doubtful question

whether the estates which he held in trust passed
under it to his devisee or not. So again, on the death
of a legal mortgagee the equitable charge devolved on
his personal representative, but the legal estate in fee
descended to his heir, or passed under his will. " The
ghost of a departed right" went wandering on from
heir to heir and from devisee to devisee, and enormous
expense was often necessary to hunt it down and get
it in; while the doubts arising in the proof of pedigrees
and the construction of a mortgagee's will, often formed
a cloud on a mortgagor's title which nothing but the
lapse of sixty years could dispel[1]. So again, on a
sale of land it was frequently necessary to prove the
vendor's pedigree, if he had inherited the land; this
would obviously have been unnecessary if the land had
vested in a realty representative. Creditors, again,
had no one to whom they could look as representing
a deceased debtor for all purposes, and it often cost
them much difficulty to ascertain in whom the legal
estate of realty was vested, and even when they had
found that person, they had no means of enforcing
their claims against him other than the "dreaded
remedy of a suit in Chancery[2]." Much confusion was
also caused by the absence of probate in wills of realty.
Of freeholds the evidence of title was the will itself;
but of leaseholds the evidence of title was the probate
and not the will.

The Ecclesiastical Commission of 1832 proposed
that probate should be required of wills of realty; but

[1] Joshua Williams, *Land Transfer*, pp. 36, 62.
[2] *Ibid.* pp. 32, 33.

the Real Property Commissioners disapproved of the proposal. They declared that nothing analogous to probate could be applied to realty unless an executor were appointed in whom the legal estate of the realty should vest; but such a measure they thought would involve far too great an interference with the law of Real Property as it then stood[1]. The proposal was repeated by the Chancery Commission of 1854 on the score of the "great and apparent advantage of the conclusive effect of probate and letters of administration in all judicial proceedings[2]." The recommendation was somewhat reluctantly adopted by Lord Cranworth in his Testamentary Jurisdiction Bill of 1854, but the project was struck out by a Select Committee, mainly at the instance of Lord St Leonards. Three years later Lord Cranworth himself opposed probate of real estate, on the ground of the substantial differences existing between realty and personalty. Personal estate, he argued, was infinite and might be distributed all over the world, and the inconvenience would be great if there was no one to represent the testator in person, no one entitled to sue for and recover all that the testator, had he been alive, might have sued for and recovered; the same necessity did not exist with regard to real estate; few persons even among the wealthy classes had more than one or two real estates, and there was no difficulty in the persons on whom real estates devolved entering on the possession without the instrumentality of any third person at all: there

---

[1] *Fourth Report*, p. 57.

[2] Second Report of Chancery Commission, *Parl. Pap.* 1854, vol. xxiv. p. 13.

was therefore no necessity to impose on real estate the costly burden of probate[1]. The Land Transfer Commission of 1854–7 nevertheless reported in favour both of probate of wills of realty and of real representatives[2]; and since the publication of their Report the establishment of real representatives has formed part of every scheme for the registration of titles to land[3]. It has been seen more and more clearly that a real representative would enormously facilitate such registration, by making the registrar less of a judicial and more of a mechanical functionary; for instead of having to determine, on a death, *who* is entitled to the property, the property would vest in the representative, and the representative would be placed on the register in the same way as an assignee in bankruptcy used to be ; and he could in his turn transfer the property to any heir, devisee or purchaser[4].

For many years—indeed until quite recently—the proposal to establish real representatives shared the fate of the Registration Bills in which it was contained. Meanwhile Parliament, *more suo,* consoled itself with piecemeal legislation. In 1859 " Lord St Leonards' Act[5] " made regulations for the sale by executors of real estate charged with the payment of debts[6]. The

[1] Lord Cranworth in Hansard, 18th May, 1857.

[2] *Parl. Pap.* 1857, vol. xviii. p. 297.

[3] It was proposed in Sir Hugh Cairns' Bill of 1859 ; in Lord Halsbury's Bills of 1887, 1888, 1889, and 1897 ; and in Lord Herschell's Bills of 1893, 1894, and 1895 ; *vide sup.* p. 69.

[4] *Parl. Pap.* 1879, vol. xi. pp. viii, ix (Osborne Morgan's Comm. Report).

[5] 22 & 23 Vict. c. 35, ss. 14, 16.

[6] On the complicated difficulties of the previous law, *vide* Williams on *Real Assets,* ch. vi.

Land Transfer Act of 1875, the Vendor and Purchaser
Act of 1874, and the Conveyancing Act of 1881[1],
removed some of the worst difficulties attending the
devolution of realty vested in trustees and mortgagees,
by providing that such realty shall devolve on the
personal representative of a deceased trustee or mortgagee, notwithstanding any testamentary disposition
thereof. The Conveyancing Act of 1881[2], lastly, empowered the personal representative of a deceased
vendor of realty to convey his land for the purpose
of giving effect to the contract of sale.

In connection with the assimilation of the intestate
descent of realty and personalty, we have now to
consider very briefly the arguments for and against
primogeniture and the postponement of females to
males, and the attempts which have been made to
change those features of our law.

To the Real Property Commissioners the law of
primogeniture appeared " far better adapted to the
constitution and habits of this kingdom than the
opposite law of equal partibility, which in a few
generations would break down the aristocracy of the
country, and by the endless subdivision of the soil
must be ultimately unfavourable to agriculture and
injurious to the best interests of the State[3]." These
two arguments—the constitution of the kingdom, and
the excessive subdivision of the soil—have to the
present day defeated all attempts to abolish primogeniture. The experience of the Continent of Europe

[1] 38 & 39 Vict. c. 87, s. 48; 37 & 38 Vict. c. 78, s. 5; 44 & 45
Vict. c. 41, s. 30.

[2] 44 & 45 Vict. c. 41, s. 4.

[3] *First Report*, p. 7.

and the opinions of economists[1] have now deprived of
all substance the latter of the two arguments. It has
also been realized that, at the worst, excessive *mor-
cellement* could easily be checked by legislative provision
of the simplest character. The same causes, too, which
have led to the present demand for the diffusion and
dispersion of land, have strengthened the case against
primogeniture. At the present day, therefore, primogeniture is defended and maintained on one ground
only, to wit, the Constitution of the kingdom; and its
days are probably numbered.

A Conservative government attempted in 1887 to
abolish primogeniture. In his Land Transfer Bill of
that year, Lord Halsbury inserted a clause making the
devolution of realty " the same as if it were personalty."
He urged its acceptance on many grounds: It would
be to the advantage of owners of property that all
property should be subject to the same legal incidents;
if an attack were made on property, it could be resisted
with much greater force if it were possible to say that
the attack included property of all kinds, and not
merely property which had any peculiar privileges.
It would be a prudent course to facilitate any system
by which land would be diffused and distributed with
advantage to both vendor and vendee; and different
laws of devolution for realty and personalty placed
difficulties in the way of the registration of title[2].
The alteration was warmly approved by Lord Herschell
and Lord Selborne, because it would remove the hard-

---

[1] *E.g.* Mill, *Political Economy*, Bk. II. ch. VII. § 5; *vide* also
Bk. v. ch. IX., where primogeniture is roundly condemned.

[2] Hansard, CCCXIII. pp. 27, 1773.

ship and the disappointment of paternal intention often inflicted by the law of primogeniture, particularly on small landholders, who alone were ever likely to die intestate; also because the change would do away with the terrors of " equitable conversion," and would, so far as it went, remove the more general and fundamental inconvenience of having two systems of property-law[1]. Lord Salisbury also consented to the abolition of primogeniture, on the rather peculiar ground that it would *not* produce the dispersion of large estates or the abandonment of the *practice* of primogeniture. He warned their lordships not to oppose the measure, without which the Land Transfer Bill would be incomplete; and he doubted whether, even if they then succeeded in rejecting it, they could cling to their victory for any considerable number of years[2]. Their lordships, however, did resist the measure; Lord Arundell of Wardour declared that primogeniture was the keystone of the institutions of the House of Lords, that the attempt to put Real Property on the same footing as Personal Property was " a sop to the Cerberus of socialism," and that the Bill if it passed would be " tantamount to a sentence of death and extinction for many ancient families[3]." The Land Transfer Bill of 1887 was shelved; on its reintroduction in 1889, the clause abolishing primogeniture was struck out in the House of Lords, but by a majority of ten votes only.

In 1892, again, Mr Cust inserted in the Small

[1] Hansard, cccxiii. pp. 32, 1767 et seqq.

[2] *Ibid.* cccxvii. p. 21.

[3] *Ibid.* cccxiii. p. 1758.

Holdings Bill of that year a clause similar to one of
the provisions of the Irish Land Purchase Act of
1891. The clause was to the effect that " small
holdings should be and should remain personal property, and should be dealt with in like manner and
be subject to like rules of law as leasehold estates[1].
The clause was adopted by the House of Commons.
It was thrown out by the Lords in Committee, but
on mere grounds of detail, viz. that it would interfere
with the operation of the Intestates' Estates Act of
1890, and that it would cause confusion to have small
portions of " personal " land intermingled with " real "
land[2].

It appears, then, that the march of events is
towards the speedy abolition of primogeniture. It is
worth while to observe that the attempts to abolish
it have not up to the present aimed further than at
the abolition of primogeniture *on intestacy*. No serious
project is as yet on foot to introduce the compulsory
partition of inheritances ; but some of those who are
most strongly convinced that the future of rural
England lies in the multiplication of small holdings,
have doubted whether the process of the aggregation
of land in a few hands can possibly be stayed so long
as freedom of bequest exists[3].

Perhaps also it is worthy of mention that in the
course of the attempts to abolish primogeniture one or
two inroads have in fact and reality been made on that
institution. Thus the Real Estates Charges Act of

[1] Hansard, IVth series, vol. v. p. 842.

[2] *Vide* Lord Chancellor Halsbury, *ibid.* p. 1428.

[3] *Vide* Lefevre, *Agrarian Tenures*, p. 289.

1854[1] (commonly known as "Locke King's Act") altered the rule of law by which an heir or devisee of mortgaged land was in general[2] entitled to have the mortgage debt paid off out of the personal property of the deceased. This rule had caused great hardships. In nineteen cases out of twenty it had defeated the intentions of the deceased mortgager, and it had sometimes reduced the widow and younger children to absolute destitution[3]. The Act, before it became law, was strongly opposed in the House of Lords on the ground that the rule which it proposed to abolish was part and parcel of the institution of primogeniture[4], but it was carried through by the efforts of Lord Cranworth, then Lord Chancellor; so that now an heir (or a devisee, unless the testator expresses a contrary intention in his will) has to take his land subject to incumbrances. The same principle was extended by an Act of 1877[5] to the case of a purchaser of land dying intestate before paying the purchase-money; under the Act, the heir of the purchaser has no longer the right to get the purchase-money paid out of the personal estate of the purchaser.

It remains to notice an isolated change made in 1890 in the devolution of both real and personal property. By the Intestates' Estates Act of 1890[6] a

---

[1] 17 & 18 Vict. c. 113, amended by 30 & 31 Vict. c. 69, and 40 & 41 Vict. c. 34.

[2] There were several capricious exceptions to the rule; Jarman on *Wills*, 1439.

[3] *Vide* Sir R. Bethell in Hansard, 18th May, 1854; Locke King, *ibid.*; and Lord Chancellor Cranworth in Hansard, 24th July, 1854.

[4] *Vide* Hansard, 31st July, 1854.

[5] 40 & 41 Vict. c. 34.   [6] 53 & 54 Vict. c. 29.

widow receives £500, in addition to her ordinary interest, on the death of her husband intestate and without children. The cases in which the Act operates are usually those in which the division of the property is between the widow on the one hand and collateral relations on the other; and the Act has increased the widow's share on no apparent principle beyond this, that the widow may reasonably be preferred by the law to collaterals, and that such a preference accords with the probable intentions of the deceased husband[1].

[1] *Vide* Lord Bramwell in Hansard, 8th July, 1890.

CHAPTER V.

MONOPOLIES.

WE now come to consider the subjectless *jura in rem* known generically as "monopolies," of which the main species recognized by English law are patents and copyrights. Though subjectless, these rights are not objectless. Their object is the same as that which forms the philosophical basis of all property, namely, to stimulate productive labour. Being *jura in rem*, being non-contractual, and being entirely distinct from the rights of the person (such as the right of personal liberty), monopolies may correctly be called proprietary rights. They are, however, distinguished from all other proprietary rights by being limited in point of duration. Though a proprietary right so limited is a curiosity in jurisprudence, the limitation is easily accounted for in the case of patents for inventions, by considerations of utility. Property in material products and commodities can be protected without interfering with the productive enterprise of others, but property in ideas cannot be protected without interfering more or less with the intellectual enterprise of others. Patent-right involves, from a practical or business point of view, a monopoly of ideas, and limits the field of invention. For this reason the duration of patent-right is strictly limited by all systems of law. The same reason explains why, in most systems of law, copyright endures for a much longer period than patent-right. Compared with patent-right, copyright involves no monopoly of ideas, nor does it narrow the field of authorship. So far as its obstructive effect is concerned, indeed, there is no reason why copyright should not be as unlimited in duration as property in material things. From this point of view, a copyright limited in duration is a curiosity in ethical as well as in analytical jurisprudence. We shall return to copyrights later; for the present, we shall give a short account of patent law and legislation.

During the last fifty years the principle of patents for inventions has been the subject of much discussion, and the most contradictory conclusions have been arrived at; nor can the controversy yet be regarded as being by any means closed. Patent-right is at present favoured by a majority of those who are competent to form a judgment. Their case may be stated somewhat as follows: A temporary monopoly is the only effectual means of stimulating invention and of overcoming the resistance which new inventions meet. A man who makes a useful invention has the right, or at any rate the *power*, of keeping that invention to himself till it dies with him, an unworked secret. He may indeed be induced to disclose the invention to the community through philanthropy, or through public spirit, or through a desire of earning admiration; but these motives operate with extreme uncertainty. The inventor, again, has it in his power to take the invention to a foreign country; and great injury is inflicted on countries giving no protection to inventors, if the native talent emigrates to countries where their invention receives better protection. In many kinds of manufacture, again, the inventor has it in his power to work his invention behind closed doors; and secrecy of manufacture is one of the greatest enemies of industrial progress[1]. For these reasons, the State makes a bargain with the inventor, in order to induce him to disclose his invention. But the inventor's monopoly exists not only in order to induce publication of inventions when made; its object is also to stimulate inventive effort. Great discoveries are seldom made by mere inspiration; they are generally the result of much labour, patient experiment and great financial expense. While the desire of benefiting their species and obtaining the approbation of their fellow-men may occasionally induce men to make such sacrifices, these motives and incentives are less efficacious than the hope and desire of individual reward. But even when the inventor has been stimulated to make an invention and to publish it, it is still necessary to place him in a privileged position, in order to enable him to introduce the invention into public use. To overcome the resistance offered to a new invention requires a long period of waiting and a large expenditure of capital. The resistance to the introduction of new inventions is often very great;—manufacturers dislike them

[1] *Vide* Resolution of International Patent Congress of Vienna, 1873, quoted in Levi, *History of British Commerce*, Part IV. ch. XII.; and C. W. Siemens, Evidence, qq. 645 et seqq. in *Parl. Pap.* 1872, vol. XI.

because they render useless existing machinery and existing methods; if the inventor were not fortified with privilege, manufacturers would often be inclined to leave well alone, and not take the risk and cost of the changes involved. Sir Charles Siemens has asserted that if a description of a new invention were found lying in a gutter, it would be in the interest of the State to pick it up and assign an owner to it in order that it might be worked[1].

For all these reasons it is necessary that a bargain should be struck between the public and the inventor. The public acquires the use of an invention which might otherwise in one way or another be lost to it. The inventor acquires a pecuniary reward, which may take one of two forms, a temporary monopoly or a direct grant of money from the State. The former has been found infinitely preferable to the latter. Grants of public money would be accompanied by all the difficulties which, as we shall see, have made it impossible to guarantee the utility of patented inventions[2]. Temporary monopolies, on the other hand, do not draw on the public purse ; and since the profits reaped from them depend on the degree in which the monopolized invention supplies the wants of the public, they possess the advantage of automatically adjusting reward to merit—the reward varies directly as the value of the invention. Inventors should therefore be rewarded by temporary monopolies in order to stimulate the making,

---

[1] *Parl. Pap.* 1872, vol. xi., C. W. Siemens, Evidence, qq. 428, 429 ; Hansard, cxviii. p. 1534 ; cclxxviii. p. 352.

[2] *Vide infra*, p. 133 ; *v.* also *Parl. Pap.* 1872, vol. xi. p. 397.

ensure the publication, and facilitate the introduction and adoption, of useful inventions. This is the case for patent-law.

The views of the statesmen, economists, and others, who desire the abolition of patent-law, may thus be summarized: In the earlier stages of mechanical invention, patents are perhaps an effectual contrivance for stimulating inventive effort; but in the present advanced development of manufacture, patents discourage instead of stimulating invention. This effect arises through the modern superabundance of patents and the multiplicity of obstructive patents. The exceedingly large number of patents taken out embarrasses the trade of a considerable class of persons, artizans, small tradesmen, and others, who cannot afford to face the expense of litigation, however weak the case of litigious patentees against them may appear to be. So large is the number of patents, again, that it has become almost impossible to ascertain what ideas are free and what are monopolized. This same circumstance produces intolerable confusion and impediment in trade and manufacture, and leads to an enormous amount of wasteful litigation; in fact, new patentees can hardly keep their feet through the litigation with which older patentees immediately assail them. On the other hand, each new invention is instantly followed by a crowd of inventions really and substantially the same, but varied and modified in shape and form for the purpose of evading the letter of the original patent.

Still greater are the evil effects of "obstructive" patents in relation both to manufactures and to the public at large. Obstructive patents are purposely made to cover as much ground as possible, so as to prevent other inventors from even approaching the subject. In a great number of cases they are so imperfectly developed that they remain inoperative and dormant themselves, while they block the way of other inventors, for of course no one will labour to give value to an invention when he knows that a patentee is lying in wait ready to reap the advantage when the practical difficulties are surmounted. Some branches of manufacture and invention are so blocked up by obstructive patents, that not only are inventors deterred from working at those branches, but the manufacturer in carrying on his regular course of business is hampered by the owners of worthless patents whom it is generally more convenient to buy off than to resist ; when an obstruction cannot be got rid of without the expense and annoyance of litigation, the manufacturer in a large majority of cases submits to an exaction rather than incur the alternative. The same obstructive tendency belongs to another common practice, viz. that of combination among a number of persons of the same trade to buy up all patents relating to it, and to pay the expense of attacking subsequent improvers out of a common fund. Even if it be granted that patent monopolies do stimulate invention, they yet affect the public interest most injuriously. By removing competition they enable the monopolist to charge a price far greater than a fair profit. The latter often finds it " better business " to sell, say, a hundred articles at an exorbitant price than a thousand at a moderate price ; by which the public loses, *pro tanto*, the benefits of the invention.

Those who hold these views propose that patents should be entirely abolished; and that in cases of exceptional merit or exceptional hardship, the State should aid the inventor with a direct grant of money[1].

Public opinion is at present decided in favour of patent-law. The facts, however, which are used in support of each of the views above described, are equally real and indisputable. One view dwells on the dark side, the other on the bright side, of patent-law. Patent-law has disadvantages as well as advantages, although the advantages appear as yet to outbalance the disadvantages. English legislation on the subject has consisted of late in an attempt to remedy as far as possible the disadvantages, while retaining the advantages, and to subordinate patent-right more completely to the interests of the public. The advantages of patent-law are greatest in the case of the most novel and valuable inventions; in proportion as inventions are less useful and original, the disadvantages of monopolizing them increase, and their multiplicity spells confusion, litigation and obstruction. Recognizing this, many eminent men have urged that the State before granting a patent should strictly examine into the novelty and the utility of the invention for which protection is claimed[2]. Since a patent, they say, is a bargain by which the public consents to bear the disadvantages incident to all

---

[1] *Vide Parl. Pap.* 1851, xviii., W. Cubitt's Evidence, q. 1547; Brunell's Evidence, q. 1774; J. L. Ricardo's Evidence, on pp. 629, 633, 635; *Parl. Pap.* 1864, xxix. p. 329 (Report of Patent Commission); *Parl. Pap.* 1871, x., Sir W. Armstrong's Evidence, qq. 2262 et seqq.

[2] *E.g.* Sir W. Armstrong, *Parl. Pap.* 1871, x. Evidence, q. 2262.

monopolies in order to acquire the use of a valuable
invention which would otherwise be lost to them,—an
investigation should be made before the bargain is
concluded, to ascertain whether the invention is worth
its price. It may have little novelty or none at all;
it may be so crude and incomplete as to be valueless
in the proposed form, and the inventor himself may
be quite incapable of bringing it to maturity; or it
may be one of that numerous class of so-called inventions which are so obvious as to be sure to present
themselves whenever attention is directed to the
subject. Others would go further, and propose that
after the investigation the State should guarantee the
novelty and the utility of the invention, in order to
prevent subsequent litigation. A bill of the year 1871
proposed to appoint Special Commissioners to examine
applications for patents, and contained provisions for
the obtaining and registration of indefeasible patents.

Both these schemes were proposed before the
Patent Law Commissions of 1851 and 1862 and before
the Select Committee of 1872[1]. The difficulties in the
way of their adoption have hitherto been considered
insuperable. No body of lawyers and scientists could
decide conclusively even on the novelty of an invention.
American experience appears to have been in this
respect conclusively unfortunate, for the Patent Ex-
aminers of the United States have continually been
found to pass old inventions as new[2]. Still more
hopeless would it be to attempt deciding on the utility,

[1] *Parl. Pap.* 1851, xviii. 633; 1864, xxix. 330; 1871, x.; 1872,
xi. qq. 431–4.

[2] *Vide* Mr Chamberlain in 1883, Hansard, cclxxviii. p. 358.

or the different degrees of utility, of inventions. The
most valuable inventions might be rejected. " The
inventive genius of a country might be stifled in
accordance with the crotchets of a few permanent
officials"; in Prussia the Bessemer process and in
Germany the Siemens process have in this way been
refused patents. "If the result of such an investigation
were to be final, the examining body would seldom
undertake the responsibility of refusing a patent; if
the examination were adequate, it would practically
involve a costly litigation in every case, instead of in
some cases; and on the whole the result would be
increased expense and delay to the patentee, with no
greater security either to him or to the public[1]."

We are now in a position to consider the patent-
legislation of the Queen's reign.

In the year 1837 the patent-law was practically in
the state in which the Statute of Monopolies had left
it. That Statute had declared monopolies void and
contrary to law, saving letters patent for the term of
fourteen years, of the sole working or making of new
manufactures within this realm, to the true and first
inventor, which others should not use at the time, so
also they were not contrary to the law or mischievous
to the State, etc.[2] Before the year 1851 no important
amendment was made of this Statute. In 1844 the
first Patent Act of the reign dealt with the case of a
patentee who had been unable to obtain due remunera-

---

[1] *Parl. Pap.* 1864, xxix. p. 330 (Report); *vide* also *Parl. Pap.* 1851,
xviii., J. L. Ricardo's Evidence, p. 633; and Mr Chamberlain in
Hansard, iiird series, cclxxviii. p. 358.

[2] 21 Jac. I. c. 3, s. 6.

tion for his expense and labour in perfecting a valuable
invention. Before 1835 such cases of hardship had
been relieved by private Acts of Parliament. A Statute
of 1835[1] provided for the extension of letters patent
for a further term of seven years on petition to Her
Majesty in Council. The Act of 1844[2] permits the
term to be extended for fourteen years where it can be
shown that an additional term of seven years will not
be long enough[3].

The stimulus given to commerce and invention by
the First International Exhibition of 1851 led to the
immediate consideration of the law of patents. Two
Patents Bills of that year were submitted in the House
of Lords to a Select Committee, which examined a
large number of witnesses not only on the then existing
defects of the English patent-law, but also on the
expediency of having a patent-law at all. The Committee reported[4] that the principal defects of the patent-
law were the delay and expense of the proceedings
necessary for obtaining a patent. The application for
a patent had to go through a number of useless offices
and stages; to the Home Secretary, to the Law Offices
of the Crown, then back to the Home Secretary, to the
three Patent Offices, the Signet Office, the Privy
Council Office, and the Office of the Great Seal. Three

[1] 5 Will. IV. c. 83, s. 4.   [2] 7 Vict. c. 69, s. 2.

[3] The Patents Act of 1883 (46 & 47 Vict. c. 57, s. 25) made no
substantial alteration in this point of the law. It merely codified
the considerations on which the Judicial Committee had previously
granted extensions. The petitioner has generally to prove two things:—
that the invention has unusual merit, and that he has been insufficiently remunerated.

[4] *Parl. Pap.* 1851, xviii. pp. 233 et seqq.

distinct patents had to be taken out for England, Scotland, and Ireland respectively. The fees were extremely high, the minimum expense of taking out a single patent being £300; this compelled poor men to have recourse to the capitalist, who naturally expected to derive some benefit from the transaction, with the result that the monopoly rights afforded by patents were not enjoyed by inventors themselves but by capitalists or middlemen. Much complaint was also made concerning the want of access to specifications of patents, and the want of protection until a patent had actually been sealed. The Committee further testified to the existence of numerous patents for inventions entirely useless, and they proposed to weed out such patents by a new method of arranging the patents fees; instead of requiring a lump sum at the beginning, they recommended that the cost of taking out a patent should be small in the first instance, but should be followed by increasing periodical payments. In this way a *locus poenitentiae* would be left to the inventor, only the fittest patents would survive to the end of the term of patent-right, and a poor inventor would be better able to protect a valuable invention till such time as he might derive profit from it.

Many improvements were effected by the Patent Law Amendment Act[1] of the following year. A single Patent Office was established, to which patentees could go for information in all stages of the proceedings; many of the stages through which applications for patents had had to pass were abolished, and practice

---

[1] (1852) 15 & 16 Vict. c. 83, amended in 1853 by 16 & 17 Vict. c. 115.

was greatly simplified. The sum total to be paid by the inventor was reduced from £300 to £175, and was made payable in three separate instalments, the smallest (£25) being paid on the granting of the patent, the next (if further protection was desired) after three years, and the last after seven years. The inventor was also enabled to take out a single patent extending over the whole of the United Kingdom.

But, as often happens when once a beginning has been made with reform, new defects were soon discovered. The multiplicity of trivial and obstructive patents was found to increase more and more. Valuable patents remained unworked or were worked insufficiently to supply the wants of the public, and a strong demand arose for compulsory licences to work such patents. Great dissatisfaction was also felt with the existing method of trying patents cases; juries seldom possessed even so much scientific knowledge as was necessary to enable them to understand the evidence, and advantage was constantly taken of their shortcomings by drawing specifications in a vague and subtle manner, by an artful generality in the form of framing the issues to be tried, and by the introduction of " a cloud of scientific evidence on the trial, to perplex rather than explain the true points at issue[1]." Many thoughtful men were so oppressed with the reality of all these disadvantages of the patent system, that they would have preferred to see that system altogether abolished. J. L. Ricardo, Kingdon Brunell, William Cubitt, and others had already in 1851 expressed such

[1] *Parl. Pap.* 1864, vol. xxix. p. 331.

an opinion[1]. In 1864 a Royal Commission, appointed
to consider the whole subject of patent-law, heard the
same view urged by a majority of the witnesses examined[2]. The conclusions ultimately formed by the
Commission did not go so far as to recommend the
abolition of patents; but they reported that "the inconveniences incident to the working of the patent-law
could not be wholly removed; they were *inherent in
the nature of a patent-law*, and must be considered as
the price which the public consented to pay for the
existence of such a law." They also affirmed that
most of the inventions patented were either trivial or
obstructive, and that in either case the patent monopoly, one of the main grounds of defence of which was
the stimulus it offered to invention, obstructed instead
of aiding the progress and improvement of arts and
manufactures[3]. The proposals of the Commission of
1864 also indicate the pessimism with which they
regarded the patent-law. They recommended that in
no case should the term of patent-right be extended
beyond the original period of fourteen years. With
regard to the cost of obtaining letters patent, they
were of opinion that large fees should be charged in
order to weed out frivolous patents which were a great
clog to subsequent inventions. They seem also to
have had a sort of feeling that the inventor sometimes
gets the best of his bargain with the public, and might
therefore justly be taxed, to redress the balance. They
recommended accordingly that no further reductions

---

[1] *Parl. Pap.* 1851, xviii. qq. 1536, 1547, 1774, and p. 629.

[2] *Ibid.* 1864, xxix. pp. 325 et seqq.

[3] *Ibid.* pp. 325, 334.

should be made in the fees of the Patent Office[1]. They decided, further, against the proposed introduction of compulsory licences to work patents; their grounds were, first, that the exceptional instances in which patentees were unwilling to grant licences did not justify a sweeping interference with rights to which the law had assigned the character of property; and, secondly, that the value of a patent and the amount of the charge that might reasonably be imposed on persons using it, varied in every instance, and it was impossible to suppose that any system of arbitration would prove satisfactory where neither precedent nor custom nor fixed rule of any kind could be appealed to on either side[2].

The recommendations of the Commission had no effect on the ensuing policy of Parliament, and the tide of public opinion soon turned strongly in favour of patent-right. A Select Committee of the House of Commons considered the whole matter in the years 1871 and 1872. They examined many witnesses, among whom were Sir William Armstrong and Sir Charles Siemens, and reported that " the privilege conferred by letters patent promoted the progress of manufactures. In the absence of the protection of letters patent the competition of manufacturers amongst themselves would doubtless lead to the introduction of improved processes and machinery, but it would probably be less rapid than under the stimulus of a patent-law[3]." At the same time the Committee

---

[1] *Parl. Pap.* 1864, xxix. p. 333.

[2] *Ibid.* 1864, xxix. p. 331.

[3] *Ibid.* 1872, xi. p. 397.

desired to see the rights of the patentee more fully subordinated to the interests both of the community at large and of other inventors; they justly denied to the patentee all right of using his privileges to the injury of the country to which he owed them. They proposed, accordingly, that letters patent should be made subject to the condition that the manufacture be carried on *within* the United Kingdom so as fully to supply the demand for the same *on reasonable terms* to the public, and with due regard to existing interests; and that letters patent should contain a clause that the patentee should grant licences on fair conditions to be determined by Commissioners[1]. The substance of the last-mentioned proposal was carried out by a provision of the Patents, Designs and Trademarks Act of 1883[2]. Under this Act the Board of Trade may order a patentee to grant licences whenever by reason of his default to grant licences on reasonable terms the patent is not being worked in this country, or the reasonable requirements of the public in respect to the invention cannot be supplied, or when any person is prevented from working or using to the best advantage another invention of which he is possessed. Potentially this provision completely protects the national interests and almost entirely removes the obstructive effect of patents. Anyone interested may petition the Board of Trade, and the Board settles the terms on which compulsory licences are ordered to be granted.

The Patents, Designs and Trademarks Act of 1883[3]

---

[1] *Parl. Pap.* 1872, xi. p. 399.   [2] 46 & 47 Vict. c. 57, s. 22.
[3] 46 & 47 Vict. c. 57, amended in minor details by 48 & 49 Vict. c. 63; 49 & 50 Vict. c. 37, and 51 & 52 Vict. c. 50.

made numerous other improvements in the patent-law. It repealed and consolidated the prior Patents Acts. It reorganized and simplified the Patent Office, and placed at its head a "Comptroller-General of Patents, Designs and Trademarks" acting under the superintendence of the Board of Trade. It reduced the total of the patents fees from £175 to £154, and made the initial payments so much lighter that twelvemonths' protection might be obtained for one pound, and four years' protection for four pounds. These fees have again been reduced by the Patent Rules of 1892, and are now payable in a series of instalments increasing annually in a mathematical progression[1]. The Act has further made provision for the exhibition of inventions at industrial and international exhibitions[2] without prejudice to the right of subsequently patenting them, and has altered the previous law by enabling executors and administrators to patent the inventions of deceased inventors[3].

With regard to foreign inventions the Act has removed a great blot from our patent-law. Soon after the passing of the Statute of Monopolies in 1624, the question arose whether a man could be called a "true and first inventor" who copied a foreign invention and brought it over into England. It was decided that although in the popular sense such a man had invented nothing, he might be a true and first inventor in the legal sense, if the invention had not been previously

[1] *Statutory Rules and Orders*, 1892, Second Set, p. 983.

[2] 46 & 47 Vict. c. 57, s. 39, amended by 49 & 50 Vict. c. 37, s. 3.

[3] 46 & 47 Vict. c. 57, s. 34.

known in England[1]. This rule of law, regarded by
Sir George Jessel as "an anomaly not depending on
any principle whatever[2]," could certainly not be justified
on the central principle of patent-law, viz. the stimula-
tion of inventive effort. It appears, however, that
there *was* a reason for such a construction of the
Statute of Monopolies[3]. The object with which patents
were granted to importers of foreign inventions was, in
an age of slow international communication, to encourage enterprising persons to go in search of and to
introduce into this country useful inventions employed
abroad, but not otherwise likely to be adopted here,
"for the want of which we should long have been
behind other nations." In modern times conditions
have changed so much as to render such a right not
only unnecessary but also unjust. There are now
great facilities of communicating with all parts of the
world ; foreign inventions are most frequently patented
in this country and in their native country simulta-
neously. The chief modern result of the anomalous
English rule has consequently been to encourage unscrupulous persons to steal the inventions of foreigners,
to run a race with the legitimate owners, and get them
patented here[4]. The Royal Commission of 1864 and
the Select Committee of 1872 urged that the law
should be changed[5], but the matter was not placed on

[1] *Vide* Jessel, M.R., in *Plimpton* v. *Malcolmson* (3 Ch. D. 555).

[2] Jessel, M.R., in *Marsden* v. *Saville Engineering Co.*, p. 205.

[3] *Vide* cases cited by Sir George Jessel in *Marsden* v. *Saville Engineering Co.*, pp. 206 et seqq.; and Report of Pat. Law Comm. 1864, *Parl. Pap.* 1864, xxix. p. 332.

[4] *Parl. Pap.* 1864, xxix. p. 332.

[5] *Ibid.* 1864, xxix. p. 333 ; 1872, xi. p. 397.

a reasonable footing before the passing of the Patents Act of 1883 and the conclusion of the International Convention for the protection of Industrial Property in the same year. The law is now that if a treaty exists with a foreign State for the mutual protection of inventions, any person who has applied for protection in that foreign State shall be entitled to a patent in England in priority to other applicants[1].

We have now finished with patents, and pass on to the kindred but in many respects different subject of copyright. The law of copyright has for two centuries been keenly discussed, and the discussion has recently been complicated through the large foreign and colonial circulation of English books, and by perplexing questions arising with regard to lectures, translations, abridgments, the dramatization of novels, etc. We shall in the main confine our attention to the national or domestic copyright of books[2], *i.e.* to the sole and exclusive liberty of multiplying copies of books in England.

It is in the interest of the public that there should be a sufficient supply of educational books, of morally instructive books, and even of books which minister to literary taste or afford other innocent enjoyment. Copyright is a temporary monopoly instituted in order to induce authors to write and publish such books. If authors were not enabled to make a livelihood out of their writings, almost the only persons to write books would be ambitious or philanthropic men of leisure;

[1] 46 & 47 Vict. c. 57, s. 103, amended by 48 & 49 Vict. c. 63, s. 6.
[2] 5 & 6 Vict. c. 45, s. 1.

poor men indeed might occasionally be inspired to write in garrets, but the slow laborious work which is equally necessary would never be undertaken in the absence of all prospect of pecuniary reward.

If a man makes an ordinary horseshoe, his ownership in that horseshoe is sufficiently protected by imposing on the rest of the community the obligation not to rob him of that horseshoe; and any other person who wishes to make a similar horseshoe has to go through the same process of heating and hammering as he did. But if a man writes a book, modern art enables others to multiply copies of that book indefinitely, at a very small expense, and without going through anything like the same process as the author. The author's interest in the book, if it is to be a proprietary right at all, can therefore only be protected by imposing on the rest of the community an obligation not to multiply copies of his book. In the absence of such an obligation, everyone would be able to print and sell copies of the book at a lower rate than the author himself could do; for the price charged by the author has to cover his outlay of time, money and labour in writing the book, and also the greater expense of printing from manuscript. In the absence of such an obligation, too, no publisher would venture to undertake the publication of the book, for anyone might undersell him as soon as it appeared probable that the book would have a successful sale.

If a man, again, makes a single horseshoe, the price which he can get for it is normally sufficient to repay his trouble in making it. But an author cannot sell a single copy of his book at a price high enough to cover

his outlay of time and labour; the conditions of literary
production are such that the author must recover both
his previous outlay and his reward in small instalments
on each sale of his book. If other persons were therefore to multiply and sell copies of the book, they would
be depriving the author *pro tanto* of his reward, and
they would *pro tanto* be reaping a reward from the
labours of the author.

On considerations such as these, a temporary monopoly has been granted to authors by the laws of all
civilized States. The author's monopoly is an evil in
so far as for a time it makes his book dearer to the
public, but the evil is cheerfully submitted to for the
sake of the greater good of getting his book at all.
Experience has shown, too, that each author is re-
strained from charging too high a price for his books
by the indirect competition which is offered by the
books of other authors. A temporary monopoly has
this immense advantage over all other means of rewarding authors, that it automatically adjusts the
amount of the reward to the acceptability of the book.
In this regard, English law has realized that a government is not a competent judge of the comparative
merits of literary productions; no books are therefore
excluded from the privileges of monopoly, except those
which can be shown to be positively injurious to morals,
religion or the political constitution of the State.

Some statesmen and many men of letters and legal
philosophers, who have approached the subject from a
more theoretical side, have come to the conclusion that
copyright should be not a temporary but a permanent
monopoly. They argue that the main utilitarian jus-

tification of all forms of property is the encouragement of productive labour. Now property in material things can be protected by giving the owner exclusive possession and enjoyment; but literary property cannot possibly remain in the exclusive possession and enjoyment of the author, the very aim and object of its production being that it should be possessed and enjoyed by the public at large. For this reason literary property is protected by forbidding the public to multiply copies of it; but in every other respect literary property possesses the same attributes as property in material things, and would be placed on the same footing by any rational Theory of Legislation. If property in material things is unlimited in duration, so ought literary property to be[1].

Others there are who maintain that there should be no copyright at all. The author, they say, has an exclusive right in his own ideas and in the form of his ideas, so long as he does not publish them to the world; but once he has published them, the ideas and facts contained in his book become part of the intellectual stock of the world, and it would be both absurd and impossible to attempt controlling their distribution and use. The copyright known to law applies only to the concrete form of words in which the author's ideas are clothed; and to that extent it is mischievous and injurious. The public interest demands that books should possess two attributes, viz. merit and cheapness. Neither of these qualities is fostered by copyright.

[1] *Vide* Huxley's and Spencer's Evidence before Royal Copyright Commission, 1878, *Parl. Pap.* 1878, vol. xxiv.; especially qq. 4833–66, 5219–76, 5552–636.

The best books are written under the stimulus of
motives higher than the prospect of gain; and under
the protection of a copyright law, books of a flimsy
and ephemeral character drive out of circulation books
of solid merit.   Copyright, again, makes books expensive; a limited sale at a high price often pays the
author better than a large sale at a lower price; the
author gains a few shillings or a few pounds, and the
public loses heavily through the restricted circulation
of the book.

Those who hold these views would substitute some
other reward for the encouragement of authors, either
some form of State-patronage, or what is known as the
" Royalty-system."   It goes almost without saying that
in our democratic days all forms of State-patronage,
even if they were feasible in practice, would be an
impossible interference with the literary choice of the
public.   As for the Royalty-system, it was disposed of
by the Royal Commission which in 1875 and the
following years considered the whole field of literary
and artistic property.   Under the proposed royalty-
system, authors were not to have the exclusive right
of publication; anyone might publish on paying to
the author a remuneration in the form of a royalty,
a definite sum prescribed by law payable to the author
for each copy published.   It was urged in favour of
this proposal that it would remove the chief evil of
monopoly—by letting in competition it would lead to
the early publication of cheap editions, and would
deprive the author of the power of issuing expensive
editions.   The Royal Commission of 1875 rejected the
proposal, on the ground, *inter alia*, that if the royalty-

system were established no publisher would take the
risk of the first publication, knowing that if the work
proved successful he would immediately have his reward
snatched from his grasp by the numerous publishers
who would republish and undersell him[1].

As we have already observed, the opinion pre-
vailing throughout the civilized world and founded
on a balance of expediency, is in favour of a temporary monopoly for authors. The Royal Copyright
Commission gave expression to this opinion when they
concluded that " in the interests of authors and of the
public alike, copyright should continue to be treated
by law as a (temporary) proprietary right, and it is
not expedient to substitute any other kind of right[2]."
Subject to this conclusion, the copyright legislation of
the Queen's reign has turned mainly on two questions,
viz., *how long* the author's monopoly ought to last, and
to what subjects it ought to extend. We shall first
consider the duration of copyright.

The copyright recognized at Common Law in the
sixteenth and seventeenth centuries was unlimited in
point of duration, but was protected only by the ineffectual remedy of an action for damages. The more
satisfactory remedies—those of fines and forfeitures—
existed under the charters and the Licensing Acts by
which the Stationers Company enjoyed a practical
monopoly of printing and publishing[3]. Consequently,
after the expiration of the last Licensing Act in 1694
authors were much discontented, and obtained in 1710

---

[1] *Parl. Pap.* 1878, vol. xxiv. p. 171.

[2] *Ibid.* p. 170.

[3] *Vide* Copinger on *Copyright*, p. 28.

the passing of an Act which fortified the old Common Law copyright with certain summary remedies. This, the earliest of all Copyright Acts, gave to authors the sole right of printing their books for the term of *fourteen years and no longer*[1], provided that after the expiration of the fourteen years the right should return to the authors, if then living, for another term of fourteen years.

After the passing of the Act it was for some time held by the Courts that the Common Law perpetual copyright had not been affected by the Act[2]; but in the great case of *Donaldson* v. *Becket*[3] the House of Lords decided (by a narrow majority and against the opinions of Lord Mansfield, Blackstone, and other learned judges[4]) that the common law copyright in published works had been altogether taken away by the Statute of Anne.

In the year 1774 authors were thus left with a bare term of fourteen or twenty-eight years. But the growth of literature soon spread a conviction that this term was far too short, and caused much sympathy to be felt with authors; popular opinion especially resented the idea that books should become public property during the author's life-time. An Act of 1814 extended the term to twenty-eight years in the first instance, and if the author was living at the end of that term then for the residue of his natural life[5].

[1] 8 Anne, c. 19, s. 11.
[2] *E.g.* in *Millar* v. *Taylor*, 4 Burrows 2303.
[3] 1774 A.D., 4 Burrows 2408.
[4] Blackstone, *Comm.* II. 407 and notes.
[5] 54 Geo. III. c. 156, s. 4.

The demands of authors and their partisans were not by any means satisfied by this. In the great literary campaign which he conducted in and out of Parliament in 1837 and the succeeding years, Serjeant Talfourd demanded a copyright term for the life of the author and sixty years after his death[1]. He declared that it was too much the tendency of the time to purchase works of a light and airy character and of temporary interest, and as such works were abundantly rewarded by immediate profits, it was the duty of the legislature to encourage that which was slow in production, high in aim, and lasting in duration, but slow to come into popular favour; that by a posthumous copyright the legislature would not only provide for the families of authors, but would give to their families and to those who cherished their memories the power of preserving the purity of their works and of securing them from pretended abridgments which would emasculate or pervert or pollute them[2].

Macaulay arose in 1841 to oppose Serjeant Talfourd, and his eloquence carried the House with him. Macaulay advocated a reasonable term of years from the publication of the book, and opposed any long extension of copyright after the author's death. He declared that the term of a life and sixty years proposed by Serjeant Talfourd far exceeded the requirements of authors, would make books unnecessarily expensive, and would be a tax on the public[3].

[1] Hansard, LVI. p. 342. He was not, however, " wedded to that term," but a less term would satisfy him.

[2] *Ibid.* LVI. p. 340. *Vide* also Hansard, XLII. pp. 555, 1703; XLV. p. 920; XLVII. p. 699; LII. p. 400.

[3] *Ibid.* LI. p. 341.

Before the next session began Serjeant Talfourd had died. His place was taken by Lord Mahon, who proposed a copyright term extending to twenty-five years after the author's death[1]. Macaulay's eloquence again won the day. In Committee he made and carried a counter-proposal to the effect that the period should be forty-two years or the life of the author, whichever should be the longer[2]. At Peel's suggestion the latter term was afterwards lengthened by seven years, and the Copyright Act of 1842[3] finally emerged to "afford greater encouragement to the production of literary works of lasting benefit to the world[4]." With this object it granted a term of copyright for the life of the author and seven years after his death, or for forty-two years from the first publication of the book, whichever term should be the longer.

Such the law has remained to the present day, notwithstanding numerous attempts recently made to extend the term of literary copyright. During the last thirty years continual and increasing complaint has been made concerning the shortness and the inconvenient mode of determination of that term. It is objected against our present law, first, that the term of copyright is not long enough. Many works, it is said, and particularly those of permanent value, are frequently but little known or appreciated for many years after they are published, and they do not command a sale sufficient to remunerate the authors until a considerable part of the term of copyright has expired; this is especially the case with works of

[1] Hansard, LXI. p. 1348. [2] *Ibid.* LXI. p. 1398.
[3] 5 & 6 Vict. c. 45. [4] Preamble of the Act.

history and philosophy, and volumes of poems. In
some instances works of these kinds have been known
to produce scarcely any remuneration until the author
has died and the copyright has nearly expired ; and
the families of many authors are left without provision
shortly after their deaths. Furthermore, the English
term of copyright is much shorter than the terms
existing in most foreign countries[1].

It is objected, secondly, that our period of copyright does not determine in a convenient manner.
There are two ways of limiting the period : either by
giving to each *book* a definite term of copyright
reckoned from the date of its publication ; or by
making the copyright of all the books written by the
same *author* to expire on a definite date such as the
death of the author or a fixed number of years after
his death. The latter system has been adopted by
European countries with hardly an exception[2]; the
present English Law combines both the systems. It
is objected to the English system, that when the
copyrights of books written by the same author expire
at different dates, it is hardly ever possible to ascertain
their termination, owing to the difficulty of verifying
the dates of publication. It is also argued that if all
copyrights were to expire at the same date, publishers
would be enabled to put out a complete edition of all
the author's works, with all the improvements and
emendations which had appeared in the later editions,
in a uniform shape and at a uniform price[3]; and lastly,

[1] *Parl. Pap.* 1878, xxiv. pp. 172–3.
[2] *Vide ibid.* pp. 173 et seqq.
[3] *Ibid.* p. 172.

that such a change in our law would greatly facilitate international copyright arrangements.

These considerations weighed heavily with the Royal Copyright Commission of 1875 already referred to. They reported that in many European countries the period of copyright was the author's life *plus* fifty years after his death, and that in most European countries the copyrights of all the books written by the same author expired on the same date[1]. They admitted that this system has a disadvantage, inasmuch as it gives a smaller reward to the later and more mature works of an author than to the crude efforts of his early life. Nevertheless they recommended that the English combination of terms should be abolished, and that a single term of a life and thirty years after death should be provided both for literary and artistic copyright; thus reverting most completely to the proposals of Serjeant Talfourd[2].

---

[1] *Parl. Pap.* 1878, xxiv. p. 173.

[2] *Ibid.* pp. 173, 174. The Commissioners also considered the *two-term* system, such as that which obtained in England before 1842. This system has certain advantages for the author, for it enables him to sell the initial term only to his publisher, and then, if he survives that term, and his book is a marked success, he, and not his publisher, profits by the second term. (*Vide* Huxley's and Spencer's Evidence, *Parl. Pap.* 1878, xxiv. qq. 5219 et seqq. and qq. 5552 et seqq.)

The Commissioners further concluded that the consequences of a *single-term* system giving an equal period of copyright to each book, would be undesirable. For besides causing difficulties as to the dates of publication, such a system might release the early and crude work of an author from copyright while he was still engaged in correcting, improving, and adding to it; which would give the earlier work an undesirable capacity of driving out of circulation the later editions.

This recommendation was embodied in government bills of 1879 and several succeeding years; but for one reason or another, and chiefly because of colonial resistance, all the bills failed. In 1891 Lord Monkswell introduced a comprehensive measure prepared by the Society of Authors under the presidency of Lord Tennyson; it was rejected as being *too* comprehensive. In 1898 the late Lord Herschell and in 1899 Lord Monkswell introduced Copyright Bills providing *inter alia* for a period of copyright of the author's life *plus* thirty years. Both bills were submitted in the House of Lords to a Select Committee which took evidence during two sessions, and lately reported in favour of the provision[1]. It is therefore probable that the period of the author's life *plus* thirty years, or some very similar period, will shortly be adopted by the legislature.

We proceed to consider the *subjects* to which copyright has been made to extend by English legislation.

The modern efficiency of mechanical and chemical processes has made it easy indefinitely to multiply copies or imitations of almost all sorts of artistic productions. Photography, chromo-lithography, the casting and moulding of materials, have done to artistic production (though sometimes in a partial and imperfect manner) what the invention of printing did to literary production. To the extent to which this is the case, a consistent code of law would evidently confer on artists a monopoly similar to the copyright of authors; provided, of course, that the State desired to encourage artistic production. The theory of the

[1] Hansard, LIV. p. 1636; LXX. p. 359. (1899 A.D.)

monopoly would in each case be based on the same
considerations, viz., the insufficient selling value of the
original production, and the possibility of indefinite
multiplication at a relatively insignificant cost.   In
applying this theory, however, to artistic production,
we find that the several forms of art arrange themselves
broadly into two classes.   The first class contains
engravings, prints, and photographs.   Copies of these
can be mechanically and chemically produced in large
numbers, and each copy is of the same, or nearly the
same, value as the original production.   These forms
of art possess all the attributes which justify literary
copyright, indeed some of them are indistinguishable
from the subjects of literary copyright; if a map, chart
or plan is protected, there seems no reason why an
engraving of a landscape should not be protected.   The
second class of artistic productions includes such higher
forms of art as paintings, drawings and sculptures.
These cannot often be reproduced with all their
original excellencies.   They can be imitated either
manually or by mechanical and chemical processes.   In
the former case the reproduction is usually more exact,
but copies cannot be multiplied with much rapidity;
the imitator, too, has to go through a great part of
the original process of production.   In the latter case
(reproduction by mechanical and chemical processes)
the reproduction is sometimes extremely imperfect;
the man who makes an engraving of a painting can,
indeed, hardly be said to " multiply copies " of the
painting.   In either case the imitation is of infinitely
less *money* value than the original work of art.   An
artist, again, who lives in a community of average

artistic proclivities can obtain for a single painting
a price sufficient to repay his outlay of time and labour;
the author of a book cannot sell a single copy for anything like that price. The second class of artistic
productions therefore possesses none of the attributes
which justify literary copyright.

Parliament, however, has drawn no distinction
between the two classes of artistic productions. Paintings and sculptures are subjects of copyright equally
with photographs and engravings. Prints and engravings were protected by Statutes of the eighteenth
century[1], sculptures by Acts of 1798 and 1814[2], paintings,
drawings and photographs by the Fine Arts Copyright
Act of 1862[3]. In the first instance this undiscriminating
legislation was probably, as Sir James Stephen suggests[4],
founded upon a mistaken view of the principle on
which the law of copyright ought to be based. In
recent years, however, copyright in paintings and
sculptures has been strenuously defended in the
interests of Art itself. The Royal Academy and the
world of art maintain that artistic copyright is necessary to the artist not only from a pecuniary point
of view, but also to enable him to insist, in the cause
of art, that the reproductions of his works shall be
creditable reproductions. Recent experience, they say,
has shown that cheap and common reproductions

[1] 8 Geo. II. c. 13 ; 7 Geo. III. c. 38 ; 17 Geo. III. c. 57.

[2] 38 Geo. III. c. 71 ; 54 Geo. III. c. 56.

[3] 25 & 26 Vict. c. 68.

[4] In a Note, appended to his signature to the Report of the
Copyright Commission of 1875, which contains some valuable ob-
servations on the theory of artistic copyright, *Parl. Pap.* 1878, vol.
XXIV. p. 219.

damage the reputation of the author and are calculated
to stop high-class reproductions; without the protection
of copyright, high-class reproductions would soon cease
to be made[1].

On these grounds not only has artistic copyright
in all its applications been maintained on the Statute
Book, but its term of duration is likely to be enlarged
by new legislation. The Copyright Commission of 1875
recommended that the term of copyright should be
made uniform for all works of fine art (photographs
excepted), and that the term should be for the artist's
life *plus* thirty years after his death[2]. The Artistic
Copyright Bill, introduced last year (1899) by Lord
Monkswell with the approval of the Royal Academy
contained a clause to the same effect. In other
respects, also, the bill proposed to fortify artistic copyright so as to " make it perfectly clear that to imitate
one form of art by another was an infringement of
copyright[3]." The bill was submitted to the Select
Committee of the House of Lords already referred to,
and was favourably received by them. It is therefore
possible that the law of artistic copyright will shortly
be amended in the direction indicated.

The law of copyright as a whole is greatly in need
of codification, or at all events, of consolidation. Many
of its rules are vague and doubtful, and they are
contained in a very large number of Statutes. Modern
literary methods continually call for new legislation.
Newspaper copyrights, lectures and sermons, abridg-

[1] *Vide* Lord Monkswell in 1899, Hansard, LXX. p. 805.

[2] *Parl. Pap.* 1878, vol. XXIV. pp. 180, 183.

[3] Lord Monkswell in Hansard, LXX. p. 806.

ments, translations, publications in magazines, the
dramatization of novels, all require legislative definition.
On all these points the Copyright Bills of the last three
years have contained provisions favourable to the rights
of the original author. The comprehensive bill prepared by Lord Herschell and Lord Monkswell proposes,
in addition, to codify and consolidate the law of
copyright[1].

Besides Patents and Copyrights, a new sort of
monopoly has been produced in the nineteenth century
through the perfection of the art of advertisement.
The right to the exclusive use of a trademark is a
jus in rem unconnected with any tangible thing; but
its principle differs from that of Patents and of Copyright. It depends on the common law rules as to
fraud and false representation; no man is allowed to
represent to the public that his goods are the goods of
another manufacturer[2].

It has long been a custom with manufacturers to
stamp their products with their names, and with
certain marks or words, as a guarantee that the
products are of their own make and of the description
represented; and great confidence is accorded to such
marks or words, especially in foreign markets. Towards
the middle of the century piracies of trademarks
occurred with great frequency. Trademarks were
counterfeited and applied to inferior articles, and all
security for the proper correspondence between the

[1] Lord Monkswell (1897) in Hansard, XLIX. p. 1594; (1898) in
Hansard, LIII. p. 461; (1899) in Hansard, LXX. p. 359; Lord Herschell
(1898), Hansard, LIV. p. 1636.
[2] James, L.J., in 18 Ch. D. 412.

article and the mark ceased to exist, and manufacturers
found themselves supplanted by inferior goods[1]. The
Courts of Equity granted a remedy by means of in-
junctions to restrain persons from using trademarks,
but the remedy was in many cases worse than the
disease. The procedure was excessively costly and
difficult; it was necessary to call large crowds of
witnesses to prove that a trademark had been "associated in the market" with the goods of a certain
manufacturer. An Act of 1862[2] made it a criminal
misdemeanour to counterfeit trademarks with intent
to defraud. In the same year a bill was brought into
Parliament for the registration of trademarks, but the
Select Committee which considered the bill reported
against registration[3]. In 1875, however, a Trademark
Act[4] made registration necessary to the acquisition
and enjoyment of an exclusive right to use a trademark.

The Act of 1875 and subsequent Trademarks Acts
have created a new method of acquiring the right to a
trademark. To benefit traders, the Acts have absolved
them (on condition of registration) from the necessity
of proving the use and reputation in the market of
their trademarks, the latest Trademark Act[5] providing
that *application* for registration shall by itself be

[1] Leone Levi, *History of British Commerce*, Pt. IV. ch. XII.
[2] 25 & 26 Vict. c. 78.   [3] *Parl. Pap.* 1862, XII. p. 431.
[4] 38 & 39 Vict. c. 91, amended by 39 & 40 Vict. c. 33, and by 40
& 41 Vict. c. 37; repealed and re-enacted by 46 & 47 Vict. c. 57;
amended by 51 & 52 Vict. c. 50.
[5] 51 & 52 Vict. c. 50, s. 17, replacing 38 & 39 Vict. c. 91, s. 2, and
46 & 47 Vict. c. 57, s. 75.

deemed equivalent to public use of the trademark. Another object of requiring registration is to protect the public, so that they may know what goods correspond to the registered trademark[1]. The Trademarks Acts have also cut down the numerous undesirable forms of words and phrases, such as names of places or common descriptive names, by which traders sought to secure to themselves exclusive rights to the detriment of other traders.

---

[1] Cotton, L.J., in L. R. Ch. D. xxxiv. 634.

CHAPTER VI.

COMMERCIAL LAW.

THE main subject of our consideration in the present chapter will be the law and the legislation concerning Companies and Partnerships. Companies and Partnerships are the most important, or at least they are amongst the most important, of the institutions which can for good or evil affect the trade and manufactures of a country. Not many years ago the extension of the co-operative principle was regarded by economists as the great economical necessity of modern industry; and it is true at the present day that the progress of the productive arts requires many sorts of industrial occupation to be carried on by larger and larger capitals, and that the productive power of industry suffers by whatever impedes the formation of large capitals through the aggregation of smaller ones[1].

The commercial law of the modern world knows in the main two sorts of business associations; they are either Corporations, or they are Partnerships.

---

[1] Mill, *Political Economy*, Bk. v. ch. ix. § 5.

A corporation is a juristic person; its essential attribute is that it is in a legal point of view distinguishable from the concrete persons composing it; it is endowed with a capacity of acquiring rights and incurring obligations; its rights and obligations are not exercisable by or enforceable against its individual members either jointly or separately, but only collectively as one fictitious whole. The purest example of a corporation known to English law is the corporation aggregate of the Common Law, the members of which are to no extent liable for the debts of the corporation; it is created either by Royal Charter or by Special Act of Parliament. The term Corporation is, however, applied also to Incorporated Companies; these usually consist of a large number of persons having transferable shares in a common fund; they are not pure corporations, for their members are more or less liable to contribute to the debts of the collective whole; they are not pure partnerships, for their members are recognized by law as an aggregate body. Incorporated Companies, in short, are intermediate between the corporations known to the Common Law, and ordinary partnerships, and partake of the nature of both[1].

The second class of business associations is generically known by the name of Partnership. The Partnership Act, 1890[2], defines a partnership as "the relation which subsists between persons carrying on business in common with a view to profit." A partnership is not a juristic person or a collective whole distinct from its concrete members, nor is it endowed

[1] Lindley on *Partnership*, p. 22.
[2] 53 & 54 Vict. c. 39, s. 1.

with any capacity of acquiring rights or incurring obligations distinct from the rights and obligations of its members. The rights and liabilities of the partnership are the rights and liabilities of the partners, and are enforceable by and against them individually, without any limitation of right or of liability[1].

Partnerships may for most purposes be divided into two classes, according to the number of partners of which they consist. First come partnerships proper or "business firms," consisting of a few members known to each other, bound together by ties of friendship and mutual confidence, and therefore not at liberty without the consent of all to retire from the firm and substitute other members in their places. The second class is constituted by Unincorporated Joint-Stock Companies, really large partnerships, formerly very common in England. They consisted of numerous partners (called shareholders), not necessarily or, indeed, usually acquainted with each other at all, so that it was a matter of comparative indifference whether changes in their *personnel* were effected or not. The law of unincorporated joint-stock companies was composed of little else than the law of partnership modified and adapted— but only in the very slightest degree—to the wants of a large and fluctuating number of members. The Courts did hardly anything in the way of adaptation. They did indeed recognize the transferability of shares of unincorporated joint-stock companies; but they insisted, on the other hand, that each member should

---

[1] *Vide* Lindley on *Partnership*, p. 21.

be liable to his uttermost farthing for the debts of the company. Both these classes of unincorporated associations have been the concern of legislators throughout the Queen's reign. The general tendency of legislation has been all in the direction of incorporation and limitation of liability, both of joint-stock companies and of small partnerships.

Early in the eighteenth century unincorporated companies with joint-stocks divided into numerous transferable shares, were already very common. The famous Bubble Act of 1720[1] declared that all associations presuming to act as corporate bodies, by the issue of transferable shares, etc., were illegal, void, and public nuisances. Joint-stock companies were, in spite of this, found indispensable to trade and manufacture, and increased in number and importance[2]. But they had to struggle against many hardships. An unincorporated joint-stock company, being really nothing more than an overgrown partnership, was practically unable to sue its debtors, and disputes between its members could not be readily, if at all, adjusted. The same difficulty was, of course, to some extent felt by all partnerships, but it particularly affected the larger partnerships known as joint-stock companies; in their case the difficulty often amounted to an absolute denial of justice. Bellenden Ker reported in 1837 that "the slightest consideration of the then existing law would show that it was absolutely inapplicable to the case of large partnerships or joint-stock companies." Of the

[1] 6 Geo. I. c. 18, ss. 18, 19.
[2] Lindley on *Companies*, p. 3.

learned witnesses examined by him "there was not one who did not fully admit the evil and urge the necessity of change[1]." An excellent example of "the evil" occurred in 1826 in the case of *Van Sandau* v. *Moore and others.* One of the shareholders of an unincorporated joint-stock company had filed a bill against the directors and the other shareholders, in order to have the partnership dissolved and the proper accounts taken. The Court held that the defendants, three hundred in number, could not be bound to answer jointly. The result of this was that the plaintiff found it impossible to proceed with a suit in which he might, as a preliminary measure, have to take office copies of three hundred answers, each with a long schedule, and where he would have to revive his suit on every alteration of the partnership by death or otherwise. Lord Eldon's observations show how unsuitable was the jurisdiction of the Court to such large partnerships. "Here is a bill," he said, "with nearly three hundred defendants; how can such a cause ever be brought to a hearing? In such a suit the plaintiff can do nothing except put himself and others to enormous expense[2]." Similar difficulties of course arose when the company was plaintiff. It became the practice, under these circumstances, for unincorporated joint-stock companies to apply to Parliament for relief in the form of Special Acts authorizing particular companies to "sue and be sued by an officer," without however absolving the

[1] *Parl. Pap.* 1837, xliv. p. 400, and *ibid.* Appendix, p. 423.
[2] 1 *Russell's Reports*, 441. Quoted by Bellenden Ker, *ubi sup.*

members from their unlimited liability[1]. These Special Acts were found to obstruct the general legislative business of Parliament, and to form a heavy tax on the finances of companies.

Such were the evils at the beginning of the Queen's reign besetting the law of large partnerships (*i.e.* unincorporated joint-stock companies). They were not only unable to limit the liability of their members, but they could not sue their debtors, and often not even their members, unless they went to the great expense of obtaining a Special Act.

A small beginning in the way of reform had been made in 1826 with regard to joint-stock banking companies, whose difficulties were the most pressing. A General Act of that year had authorized them to sue and be sued in the name of a public officer[2]. But no serious step was taken till the year 1837, when the Committee for Trade of the Privy Council directed Bellenden Ker to inquire into the state of the law of partnership, " more especially as regarded the difficulties of suing and being sued when partners were numerous." Ker's report, presented in the same year,

---

[1] " A Company," says Lindley, L.J., " which without being incorporated is privileged to sue and be sued by the name of some public officer, is as it were halfway between an incorporated and an unincorporated company. So far as its privileges do not make a difference, the company is a partnership; so far as its privileges extend it may without any great inaccuracy be likened to a corporation, for the main object of these privileges is to confer on the company a sort of continuous existence, whatever changes may take place among its individual shareholders." (Lindley on *Companies*, p. 2.)

[2] 7 Geo. IV. c. 46, amended by 1 & 2 Vict. c. 96; 3 & 4 Vict. c. 111; 5 & 6 Vict. c. 85, and 27 & 28 Vict. c. 32.

contained the evidence of several eminent merchants,
bankers, and lawyers[1]. With regard to partnerships
"where the partners were numerous," he made several
recommendations on which was founded the Letters
Patent Act of 1837[2]. This Act empowered the Crown
to grant by letters patent to such partnerships or
companies the right of suing and being sued in the
name of an officer, without, however, incorporating the
company; it also empowered the Crown in certain cases
to limit to a given extent the liability of the members
of such companies. The Act was not a success. It
was defective in not affording the public any means of
information concerning the constitution or the limitation of liability of companies chartered by letters patent
under its terms. The procedure for obtaining charters
was excessively tedious and expensive, especially if any
limitation of liability was desired. The great majority
of joint-stock companies took no advantage of the Act.
They remained unincorporated and charterless. In
remaining so, they were often actuated by questionable
or fraudulent motives; the opening years of the reign
were marked by an epidemic of Bubble Companies
similar to that which had led to the Bubble Act of
1720. In 1841 and in 1843 Select Committees of the
House of Commons took abundant evidence concerning
the "modes of deception adopted by these charterless
companies, the amount and distribution of the plunder,
the circumstances of the victims, and the impunity of
the offenders." They reported[3] that the evil was wide-

---

[1] *Parl. Pap.* 1837, XLIV. from page 399.

[2] 7 Will. IV. & 1 Vict. c. 73.

[3] *Parl. Pap.* 1844, VII. from p. 1.

spread. The victims were usually persons of limited
means, who invested their savings in order to obtain
the tempting returns which were offered, such as gover-
nesses, servants and old people; sometimes persons of
more property and better intelligence were tempted.
The "concoctors" of a fraudulent company, however
largely they had despoiled the public, were practically unamenable to any jurisdiction whether civil or
criminal. The victims of their frauds usually found
it impossible to discover of whom the company consisted. Even if they made that discovery, they were
generally so impoverished by their losses as not to
be able to pursue the offenders, or so ashamed of
being involved in the transaction as to be disinclined
to expose themselves by doing so. Even if they were
able and willing to prosecute, the legal proceedings
open to them were, as we have observed, almost
nugatory. If proceedings were taken in Chancery,
each defendant was entitled to proceed by separate
answer, and the suit usually broke down; criminal
proceedings it was equally difficult to sustain, by the
lack of the necessary evidence. Offenders, even if
baffled in one concern, availed themselves of the
general impersonal designation of companies to start
others equally objectionable, and no possibility existed
of apprising the public of the identity of the company.

The Committee came to the resolution that in order
to prevent the formation of fraudulent companies, and
to protect the interests of shareholders and of the
public, all joint-stock companies (other than banking
companies) ought to be registered in a public office;
and they recommended that the registration should

include the name and purpose of the company; its place of business; the names, addresses and occupations of promoters, directors, patrons, other officers, and members; and the amount of nominal capital and the proportion paid up. The resolution was immediately adopted in an Act of Parliament of 1844[1] which provided for the registration of all trading joint-stock companies. The effect of registration under the Act was to incorporate the company, but without in any way limiting the liability of its members[2].

The Act was a great failure. It did indeed render some forms of fraud more difficult; but, on the other hand, it gave the guarantee (so considered by the public) of incorporation to companies with unlimited liability. This was a most unfortunate thing, especially

[1] 7 & 8 Vict. c. 110, amended by 10 & 11 Vict. c. 78, repealed by 25 & 26 Vict. c. 89.

[2] An Act (7 & 8 Vict. c. 113, repealed by 25 & 26 Vict. c. 89) of the same session provided for the incorporation of banking companies, for a term of twenty years by letters patent, but without any limitation of liability. The Banking Legislation of the period, including "Peel's Act" of 1844, is described in Bagehot's *Lombard Street*, chap. III.

In the following year (1845) three General Acts (Companies Clauses Act (8 & 9 Vict. c. 16); Land Clauses Act (8 & 9 Vict. c. 18); Railway Clauses Act (8 & 9 Vict. c. 20)) were passed which have effected much saving of expense in the incorporation of companies by Special Acts. Special Acts are still necessary for the formation of companies to carry on undertakings of a public nature, especially when compulsory powers of purchasing land, etc., are required. It was thought expedient to comprise, in the General Acts referred to, sundry provisions relating to the constitution and management of public companies, usually introduced into Special Acts; the objects being to avoid the necessity of repeating such provisions in each of the Special Acts, and to secure greater uniformity in the provisions themselves. In both these objects the Acts have been completely successful.

unsuited to the circumstances of the time. The period
of Peel's free-trade measures was one of great improvement in the economic condition of the people. There
was a great increase in the amount of personal property.
Since the beginning of the century the urban population
of England, chiefly dependent on personal property, had
grown at the rate of thirty per cent. in every decennial
period. In the thirty-three years following the great
peace of 1815, houses, factories, and warehouses, owned
by persons depending on trade and commerce, had
augmented twenty-six million pounds in annual value.
Most of this personal wealth was distributed among
the middle and working classes of the population;
these classes grew in numbers and importance; there
was a large increase in the number of depositors and
the amount of deposits in Savings Banks, and in the
number of persons receiving under £5 at each payment
of dividends on the public debt; there was a much
larger income, between £150 and £500, assessed to
income tax[1]. There was, in short, a large surplus of
capital in quest of promising employment. But there
were no increased facilities for safe investment. The
middle classes much desired investments in land or on
mortgage, but were deterred by the uncertainty of titles
and the expense of conveyances[2]. The only field for
investment was that offered by the incorporated companies with unlimited liability registered under the
Act of 1844[3]. A period of reckless speculation set in,
especially with iron, cotton and railway shares. In 1846
there was a Railway mania; no fewer than twelve

[1] *Parl. Pap.* 1851, xviii. p. 1.
[2] *Ibid.* 1850, xix. p. 169.   [3] 7 & 8 Vict. c. 110.

hundred and sixty railway schemes were launched,
with a total proposed expenditure of £560,000,000[1].
In 1847 followed one of the greatest commercial crises
ever known; the unlimited liability of the wild-cat
Railway companies involved in utter ruin thousands
who had no financial knowledge or experience. In
1850 Mr R. A. Slaney obtained from the House of
Commons a Select Committee to consider the subject
of "investments for the savings of the middle and
working classes." Having examined many witnesses,
amongst whom were Mill and Bellenden Ker, the Committee reported that the Crown was indeed empowered
by the Letters Patent Act of 1837 in certain cases to
limit the liability of partners (*i.e.* of joint-stock companies), but that this power was seldom exercised, did
not seem to be guided by any clear rule, and involved
expense greater even than that of obtaining a Special
Act of Parliament. They further observed that the
state of the law opposed obstacles to the improvement
of the working classes, especially by hindering co-operative associations in industry; the law gave no effectual
remedy against the fraud of a dishonest contributor or
partner, and no summary mode of enforcing the rules
agreed to for mutual government[2]. Political economists
at that time entertained high hopes of the educative
and industrial advantages of co-operative association[3],
and the representations of the Committee, repeated by
another Committee in the following year[4], brought

[1] Levi, *History of British Commerce*, Part IV. ch. v.

[2] *Parl. Pap.* 1850, XIX. p. 171.

[3] Mill's Evidence, *Parl. Pap.* 1850, XIX. qq. 837 et seqq., and Mill,
Political Economy, Bk. v. ch. IX. § 7.

[4] *Parl. Pap.* 1851, XVIII. p. 3.

about the Industrial and Providential Partnerships Act of 1852. This Act admitted industrial associations to the statutory privileges of Friendly Societies, exempted them from the formalities applicable to other joint-stock companies, and provided for the settlement of disputes among their partners without having recourse to the Court of Chancery.

In 1851 Mr Slaney obtained another Select Committee to consider the law of partnership and the "expediency of facilitating the limitation of liability with a view to encouraging useful enterprise and the additional employment of labour." The Committee took much evidence from Mill, Babbage, Bellenden Ker, Leone Levi and others. They reported testifying to the great increase of wealth, and its distribution among large numbers of the people "in the middle or even the humbler ranks of life"; and to the difficulty and expense, and in some cases the impossibility, of obtaining charters for limiting the liability of companies[1].

Their recommendations were divided under the two headings of *large* partnerships and "*small* or *ordinary* partnerships." The history of small partnerships we shall consider later. With regard to large partnerships, they proposed that greater facilities should be afforded for obtaining charters. For useful enterprises like waterworks, roads, and reading-rooms, they advised a limitation of liability; they thought it "would be a subject of regret if cautious persons of moderate capital and esteemed for their intelligence should be deterred

---

[1] *Parl. Pap.* 1851, xviii. pp. 3, 6.

from taking part in such undertakings by the heavy
risk of unlimited liability." On the question of introducing limited liability among joint-stock companies
generally, the witnesses examined gave the most
conflicting evidence. Some strongly opposed the idea,
fearing that the public would be deceived into giving
credit beyond the sum of the capital paid up or
guaranteed by the shareholders of a company, and
that there would be less security against reckless
speculation, the speculator knowing that he did not
risk his whole fortune on the speculation. Others
favoured it, maintaining that no danger would exist
under a suitable system of registration and with sufficient publicity given to the affairs of the company, and
that with such safeguards a company would find it
practically impossible to speculate beyond the bounds
of its ordinary course of business, or beyond the limits
of its capital reserve.

The recommendations of the Committee were most
liberally interpreted by the majority in Parliament.
A Bill was introduced for enabling joint-stock companies to be registered and incorporated with limited
liability. In the ardent debates which followed, it was
argued in favour of the Bill that companies with
limited liability gave great satisfaction in France, the
United States, and the Low Countries; that their
introduction into England would allow small capitalists
to combine to the extent of their limited capital to
prosecute many branches of trade with advantage to
themselves and to the public; that it would give the
working classes a chance of profitably investing their
savings; and that a great quantity of small capital had

formerly been locked up, which, if the Bill passed, might be employed for the benefit of all concerned. Those who opposed the Bill contended that if America had prospered under the law of limited liability, they could not anticipate that the same would happen in England, for in America capital was extremely scarce, whereas in England there was no want of capital; that men having some capital would invest it in undertakings of the nature of which they would be totally ignorant, and would have to intrust the sole management of their property to a body of directors who instead of being the servants would be the masters of the company; that the Bill would entrap persons into improvident and dishonest speculations; that under a law of limited liability a man might be a bankrupt in one street, and a merchant prince round the corner in another concern, which was "irreconcile-able with sound morality[1]."

The Bill, nevertheless, became the Limited Liability Act of 1855[2]. The Act was amended in 1856; in 1857 it was amended and its privileges extended to banking companies; it was repealed and re-enacted with amendments by the Companies Act of 1862, which also consolidated the whole of the company law. The Act of 1862[3] completed the conversion of joint-stock companies from merely large partnerships into corporate bodies, by providing that if more than twenty-one (or

---

[1] *Vide* Hansard, cxxxix. pp. 1378, 1445, 1895.

[2] 18 & 19 Vict. c. 133; 19 & 20 Vict. c. 47; 20 & 21 Vict. c. 14; 20 & 21 Vict. c. 49; amended by 20 & 21 Vict. c. 80; 21 & 22 Vict. c. 60, and 21 & 22 Vict. c. 91.

[3] 25 & 26 Vict. c. 89.

in the case of bankers, if more than ten) persons associate to carry on business for the acquisition of gain, they must register themselves as a company. The compulsion thus applied by the Act was intended to prevent the mischief which, as we have seen, arose from the carrying on of commercial undertakings by bodies so large and fluctuating that persons dealing with them did not know with whom they were contracting, and so might be put to great difficulty and expense[1].

Since the year 1862 legislation concerning companies has been in the way of elaboration rather than of change[2]. It has in the main been directed to two objects, viz. to protect the public against the misrepresentations, and shareholders against the frauds, of company directors and promoters, and secondly to provide for the winding up of insolvent companies in a manner equitable alike to creditors, shareholders and ex-shareholders. The latter object has been successfully achieved by the Companies Winding-up Act[3] of 1890. With regard to the former object an Act[4] of the present year (1900) attempts to prevent the *formation* of fraudulent companies rather than to inflict pains and penalties on directors and promoters after the event. The Act[5] provides against the evil of directors acting without qualification or taking gifts of

[1] *Vide* also James, L.J., in *Smith* v. *Anderson*, 15 Ch. D. 273.

[2] 30 & 31 Vict. c. 131; 40 & 41 Vict. c. 26; 42 & 43 Vict. c. 76; 43 & 44 Vict. c. 19; 46 & 47 Vict. c. 28; 53 & 54 Vict. c. 62, and 53 & 54 Vict. c. 63.

[3] 53 & 54 Vict. c. 63.   [4] 63 & 64 Vict. c. 48.

[5] ss. 2, 3.

unpaid shares, against fictitious subscriptions[1], against secret payments to promoters and vendors of shares[2]; it provides for a minimum proportion of capital to be actually paid up before a company commences business[3], contains stringent requirements as to the contents of prospectuses, and secures publicity to certain mortgages of the property of companies[4].

At the present day no doubt is entertained as to the beneficial effects of the company-law constructed in the course of the Queen's reign. "The Companies Acts," says Mr Palmer, "have stimulated and developed British trade and co-operative enterprise in all parts of the world. The paid-up capital of companies under the Act of 1862, together with debentures and debenture stock, now amounts to something like sixteen hundred millions sterling[5]."

We may now take leave of large partnerships or joint-stock companies, and proceed to consider the history of those small or ordinary partnerships which are commonly known as business firms.

The English law of partnership has always been much better adapted to the small partnerships with a view to whose regulation it was originally created, and the law concerning small partnerships has been proportionately free from legislative interference. Towards the end of the eighteenth century, however, and in the beginning of the nineteenth, much discussion took place about the expediency of introducing the principle of *commandite* into that law[6]. Partnership

[1] ss. 4, 5. [2] s. 6. [3] s. 10. [4] s. 14.
[5] Palmer on *Companies*, p. 10.
[6] *Parl. Pap.* 1837, XLIV. from p. 399.

en commandite according to the French *Code du Commerce* is a contract between one or more partners responsible for themselves and for each other, and one or more partners simply depositors of capital, who are called *commanditaires* or partners *en commandite*; and a partner *en commandite* is not liable for losses beyond the extent of the funds which he contributes or has undertaken to contribute to the partnership capital[1]. It is to be understood however that the partner *en commandite* is not *merely* a lender of money at a rate of interest varying with the profits of the partnership business; he is a real partner whose powers and liabilities are limited[2]. Partnership *en commandite*, which was well known in the medieval commerce of the Mediterranean, was regulated in the year 1673 by an ordinance of Louis XIV., and has since that date been adopted by all commercial nations, England only excepted[3]. The tendency of English judges rather was in the beginning of the nineteenth century to hold that whoever in any way shared the profits of a partnership business must be a partner, and therefore liable for all the partnership debts, any contrary agreement notwithstanding, and whether or not he described himself as a mere creditor. Partnerships were much hampered by this rigorous judiciary law, which, in combination with the usury laws, made it almost impossible for an embarrassed firm to obtain loans of money on any terms.

[1] *Code du Commerce*, Arts. 23, 26.

[2] Sir F. Pollock, *Jurisprudence and Ethics*, p. 95.

[3] *Ibid.* from p. 95. It was introduced into Ireland by the Anonymous Partnership Act (Irish Stats. 21 & 22 Geo. III. c. 46).

Under these circumstances, Bellenden Ker was appointed in 1837 to consider *inter alia* whether it would be expedient to introduce anything similar to the French law of partnership *en commandite*. Ker himself and most of the authorities whom he consulted were adverse to its introduction[1], and nothing more was heard of the matter till 1851. In the latter year Mr Slaney's Select Committee, already referred to, considered the law of partnership. With regard to commandite partnership or "limited" partnership (synonymous) they reported that the witnesses examined by them were much divided on the subject, and that it would require great care to devise the checks and safeguards against fraud, necessary to accompany the introduction of commandite partnership into England. They therefore proposed very cautiously with regard to the important and much controverted question of the limited or unlimited liability of partners, a Commission should be appointed of adequate legal and commercial knowledge to suggest such changes in the law as the altered condition of the country required[2].

In accordance with this proposal, the Royal Mercantile Law Commission appointed in 1852 was in 1853 requested to consider the expediency of introducing commandite partnership. They reported in 1854 against its introduction, by a majority of five to three[3]. The question of paramount importance, they declared, was whether commandite partnership

[1] *Parl. Pap.* 1837, xliv. from p. 399.
[2] *Ibid.* 1851, xviii. Report from p. 1.
[3] *Ibid.* 1854, xxvii. p. 447.

would operate beneficially on the general trading interests of the country. The conclusion to which they had arrived was that it would not; for on the one hand there was in England no lack of capital for the requirements of trade, and on the other hand such partnerships would increase the danger of fraud, and would therefore be prejudicial to our mercantile reputation. They considered moreover that the benefit which commandite partnership might confer on individuals by enabling them to obtain capital and establish themselves in business by the aid of partners incurring a limited liability only, had been greatly overrated; and that the advantage to be acquired either by the commandite or by the managing partners would be at the expense of a more than countervailing amount of injury to traders bearing the burden of unlimited liability, who would have to compete with them.

These plausible rather than convincing arguments were stoutly opposed by the three dissenting Commissioners[1]. The conclusion to which *they* had come was that commandite partnership was capable of fulfilling certain industrial functions which could not be equally well fulfilled by any other form of business association, not even by joint-stock companies with limited liability. This conclusion has been, and is, shared by many eminent statesmen, lawyers, economists and commercial men; by Mill, Bouverie, Babbage, and Sir Frederick Pollock. The arguments on which it

[1] Mr (afterwards Baron) Bramwell, Mr James Anderson, and Mr Kirkman D. Hodgson.

rests have been continually repeated both in and out of Parliament; they may be thus shortly stated:

No one can consistently condemn commandite partnership without being prepared to maintain that no business should be carried on with borrowed capital; in other words, that the profits of business should be wholly monopolized by those who have had the time to accumulate or the good fortune to inherit capital; a proposition in the present state of commerce and industry evidently absurd. The introduction of commandite partnership would lead to a substantial increase in the amount of capital engaged in industry and commerce, and would enable young men and beginners in business to obtain capital. It would moreover enable a partnership business to be continued on the death or retirement of one of the partners, for the retiring partner (or his executor) would be perfectly content to allow a large proportion of his money to remain in a concern which he knew to be thriving and profitable, on the condition of receiving a share of the profits, in lieu of obtaining interest for his money from other sources. It would also enable capitalists to help inventors in the way in which the latter may best be assisted; in order to obtain advances of money, an inventor could offer to make the capitalist a commandite partner; in the absence of that power it is extremely difficult for an inventor to find a capitalist willing to risk his whole fortune on the success of an invention. Under a proper system of registering the names of the commandite partners and the amount of their contributions or liabilities to contribute, the public at large would have ample notice of the fact

that the affair is a commandite partnership; the abuse
of credit would not be encouraged but rather discouraged. Commandite partnership, furthermore, has
been adopted and found satisfactory by every civilized
country except England, and great inconveniences
result from the fact that our law on this point is
different from that of all other countries. It was also
formerly argued with more force than at present that
commandite partnership would allow capitalists to help
co-operative or industrial societies, to the mutual
benefit of all concerned, by coming in as commandite
partners; and Mill condemned the English law of
partnership as being inconsistent with the payment of
wages in part by a percentage on the profits, in other
words, with the association of operatives as virtual
partners with the capitalist[1] (the " Profit-sharing "
scheme).

In spite of the unfavourable report of the Mercantile
Law Commission, Sir R. P. Collier in 1854 moved a
resolution in the House of Commons " That the law of
partnership which rendered every person who shared
the profits of a trading concern liable to the whole of
its debts, was unsatisfactory and should be so far
modified as to permit persons to contribute to the
capital of such concerns on terms of sharing their
profits, without incurring liability beyond a limited
amount[2]." The resolution led to a long debate, in

---

[1] *Vide Parl. Pap.* 1850, vol. xix. qq. 847–9; Babbage's Evidence
in *Parl. Pap.* 1851, vol. xviii. p. 183; Mill's Evidence, *ibid.* p. 182;
Parl. Pap. 1854, vol. xxvii. p. 453; Hansard, iiird series, cxxxix.
p. 310; *Parl. Pap.* 1882, vol. xii. pp. 331, 335; and Mill, *Political
Economy*, Bk. v. ch. ix. § 7.

[2] Hansard, cxxxiv. p. 756.

which it was apparently assumed on all hands that it contemplated the introduction of commandite partnership (which it did not). The debate ended in a promise by Lord Palmerston that the Government would seriously consider the matter[1]. In 1855 and 1856 bills were introduced by Mr Bouverie, this time with the unmistakeable object of establishing commandite partnership[2]. The bills proposed that two sorts of partners should be recognized by the law, "general" partners and "limited" partners, and that partnerships containing limited partners, together with the shares of the limited partners, should be registered by the Registrar of joint-stock companies. The proposal was violently opposed on the grounds that M'Culloch the political economist disapproved of limited liability except in the case of very large concerns like railway or canal companies; that there was enough capital in the country; and that the proposal would lead to reckless speculation[3]. By the House in general the proposal was favourably received, and would probably have become law, had it not been for the overshadowing influence of the Report of the Mercantile Law Commission. Similar bills were unsuccessfully introduced in 1862, 1863, and 1864[4]. The attempt to establish commandite partnership was then abandoned, and in 1865 a less ambitious bill was brought in, became law, and is known as "Bovill's Act[5]."

[1] Hansard, cxxxiv. p. 800.

[2] *Ibid.* cxxxix. pp. 310–358; and *Parl. Pap.* 1856, v. pp. 373, 381.

[3] Hansard, cxxxix. pp. 636, 1350.

[4] *Parl. Pap.* 1862, iv. p. 55; 1863, iii. p. 203; 1864, iii. p. 197.

[5] 28 & 29 Vict. c. 86.

Bovill's Act did not introduce commandite partnership, or anything like it, into the English law. It merely removed the hardship of the rigorous judiciary law that whoever shared the profits of a business was liable as a partner. It did not introduce contributing partners with limited liability and with limited powers of doing partnership business, nor did it introduce any system of registering the contributions of the limited partners. It merely enacted that if a person lends money to a trading concern at a rate of interest varying with its profits, he shall *not* thereby become a partner, limited or unlimited; although if the concern becomes bankrupt, he cannot recover his loan until the claims of other creditors have been satisfied. It was therefore entirely wrong to suppose (as was supposed) that the Act introduced the main principles of commandite partnership into the English law[1]. Owing to this supposition, great benefits were expected from the Act, but the expectation has been grievously disappointed. "What happens in practice," says Sir Frederick Pollock, "since the passing of Bovill's Act, is that the lender who advances his money for a share of the profits is not content to be a passive creditor. He enters into an agreement by which his so-called loan is completely embarked in the capital of the

[1] Another curious point about the Act, noticed by Sir Frederick Pollock, is that the common law rule which it purported to abolish had in fact been abolished five years before by the judges themselves in the case of *Cox* v. *Hickman* (1860 A.D., 8 H.L.C. 312). "Parliament intended to produce a substantial amendment of the law, and produced unawares a stray bit of codification." (Pollock, *Digest of the Law of Partnership*, pp. 17, 21; *Jurisprudence and Ethics*, ch. III. p. 83.)

business, and he receives in return most of the rights and powers of a partner as between himself and the nominal borrower. Then, if the business fails, he finds that notwithstanding Bovill's Act he is liable as a partner, with *unlimited* liability." The Act has failed in another respect. It has introduced one of the chief dangers of commandite partnership, for it enables a trader to defraud the public by passing off borrowed capital as his own, and obtaining credit on it; while it is unaccompanied with the safeguard by which true commandite partnership guards against this danger, viz. the compulsory registration of the commanditaire partners and of the amount of their contributions and liabilities[1].

This being so, it is not surprising to learn that since 1865 the attempt to introduce commandite partnership has been continually renewed. In 1879 Sir Frederick Pollock drafted a bill to introduce commandite partnership, to provide for the compulsory registration of *all* partnerships, and to codify the existing partnership law, with the exception of that part of it which is involved in the law of bankruptcy. So much of the bill as dealt with compulsory registration of partnerships was soon dropped because of the opposition of the Board of Trade[2]. The remaining portion of it was in 1882 submitted to a Select Committee of the House of Commons which struck out the provisions relating to commandite partnership.

---

[1] *Essays in Jurisprudence and Ethics*, ch. IV. p. 103.

[2] The question of the registration of partnership firms in general is sketched by Sir F. Pollock in *Jurisprudence and Ethics*, ch. IV. from p. 106.

The latter institution is nevertheless bound sooner or later to make its appearance in our law. The presumption is very strong that we "lose something by not possessing what has been found useful by many mercantile communities." We have at any rate Sir Frederick Pollock's testimony, founded on the actual experiment of drafting a bill, that "the technical difficulties of making the commandite system fit in with our existing law of partnership, are not of a really formidable kind[1]."

The rest of the bill mainly aimed at turning into statute-law the case-law of which the law of partnership consisted; that is to say, it was a codifying measure. Sir Frederick Pollock declares that "in England we never get a code or any chapter of a code by force of pure argument; we must make it clear that a strong body of persons are interested in the thing being done, want it done, and see their way clear to doing it." With regard to the codification of partnership law these conditions were amply fulfilled. The commercial world had made up its mind that an authentic consolidation of the law of partnership was desirable[2]. The codifying bill was more than once introduced between 1882 and 1887 without reaching the stage of effectual debate; but in 1888 and 1889 it was seriously considered by the Board of Trade. In 1890 it was introduced in the House of Lords, which made some amendments; it passed through the Commons with a few more amendments, and

---

[1] *Jurisprudence and Ethics*, p. 102.

[2] *Ibid.* p. 98.

became the Partnership Act of 1890[1]. This Act does
not purport to be a complete and exclusive codification
of the law of partnership, one of its sections[2] providing
that the rules of equity and common law applicable to
partnership shall continue in force except in so far as
they are inconsistent with the express provisions of the
Act.   Of the few changes which the Act introduces
into the law, the most important is the provision
that execution shall not issue against any partnership
property except on a judgment against the firm.
Previously, partnership property could be taken in
execution for the separate debt of a partner, and the
sheriff had to sell that partner's interest in the goods
seized, although it was generally impossible to ascertain
what that interest was except by taking the partnership
accounts; which had caused much inconvenience[3].   For
the rest, the Act has made the law more accessible, and
has greatly lessened the necessity of verifying old
authorities.   But it has not removed that necessity
altogether; "Should any practitioner imagine that he
may now relegate Lord Justice Lindley's book to an
upper shelf, he would soon be undeceived.   Codes are
meant not to dispense lawyers from being learned, but
for the ease of the lay people and the greater usefulness
of the law[4]."

The same observation would apply to two other
Statutes which have recently codified two great departments of our commercial law.   The first is the

---

[1] 53 & 54 Vict. c. 39.   [2] s. 46 of the Act.

[3] Pollock, *Digest of Law of Partnership*, p. 69.

[4] *Ibid.* p. viii.

Bills of Exchange Act of 1882[1], of which Judge Chalmers was the draftsman. This Statute has had the most successful result, not only in rendering the law more accessible, but apparently also in diminishing litigation on the law codified by it[2]. Another and an unexpected advantage has been derived from the codification of the law of bills of exchange; the codifying Act has been adopted by New Zealand, New South Wales, South Australia, Victoria, Queensland, Tasmania, and the Dominion of Canada, so that there is now a uniform code on a most important branch of commercial law in the mother country and in the greater proportion of her self-governing colonies[3].

The other codifying Statute is the Sale of Goods Act of 1893[4]. In drafting the Sale of Goods Bill Judge Chalmers reproduced as exactly as possible the existing law, leaving all amendment to the discretion of Parliament. The changes consciously made by the Act, other than the settling of doubtful points, are very slight[5].

The results of the three codifying Acts have on the whole been most encouraging. It is most probable,

[1] 45 & 46 Vict. c. 61.

[2] Lord Herschell in Hansard, cccxxx. p. 70 (1893 A.D.).

[3] *Ibid.* cccxxxi. p. 1181. Very few substantive changes were made by the Act; perhaps the most important is that contained in s. 8, sub-s. 4, by which a bill or note is made negotiable when it does not contain words prohibiting transfer or indicating an intention that it should not be transferable.

[4] 56 & 57 Vict. c. 71.

[5] The chief are, in s. 18, rules 2 and 3, the words "and the buyer has notice thereof"; and, in s. 24, sub-s. 2, the alteration of the prior law as to the effect of conviction in re-vesting property of goods obtained by fraud or wrongful means not amounting to larceny.

as Lord Herschell[1] once declared, that a progressive codification of "ripe branches of law" is the only means of accomplishing a general codification of the law of England. The instalment system has also the advantage of allowing a minute care and attention which is extremely desirable but which is only possible when isolated departments of the law are separately dealt with.

[1] Hansard, cccxxx. p. 70.

CHAPTER VII.

DEBTS AND SECURITIES.

In this chapter we shall consider historically the means by which a creditor may in the last resort appeal to the State to use physical force in order to satisfy his debt out of the property of his debtor, the limitations placed by law on the personal and proprietary liabilities of a debtor who has not the wherewithal to pay his creditors, and the contractual methods by which a creditor may render a determinate portion of his debtor's property available for the payment of his demands in priority to those of other creditors. We shall consider the rights of the creditor in the following order:—first, the laws of judgment and execution against the property of a living debtor; secondly, the distribution of the property of a deceased debtor; thirdly, the law of bankruptcy; and lastly, the law of contractual securities.

Partly through the mere lapse of time, partly as a consequence of the fact that the legislature was a body of landholders, the laws of judgments and execution were at the commencement of the Queen's

reign in a most unsatisfactory state. The creditor who
had obtained a favourable judgment in a court of law
found himself provided with the most ineffectual means
of enforcing it. In some respects indeed his powers
were unnecessarily wide and injurious to others besides
his debtor, but for every proper and useful purpose his
remedies were absurdly inadequate. As Lord Chancellor
Cottenham observed in 1838, "the creditor had the
power against the body of his debtor which he ought
not to have, while he had not the remedy against the
property of his debtor which he ought to have[1]."

A debtor could be thrown into prison by his creditor
on mesne process, before a judicial decision or anything
in the nature of a judicial decision had taken place.
Personal liberty was a most precarious attribute;
anyone might be summarily imprisoned if anyone else
would make an affidavit that he owed him twenty
pounds. By a curious perversion, our law presumed that
in an action for debt the defendant was not only in the
wrong, but was also meditating flight from his home
and his country[2]. Brougham feelingly complained that
"if a gentleman bought twenty pounds' worth of goods
on a Saturday, went to his villa, and returned on
Monday, on knocking at his door he might be met with
an arrest, and he must accompany the sheriff's officer
to a lock-up house. He would then usually send for
his butcher and his baker, and get bailed; but a
gentleman could not after that complain so well of the
meat or the bread, or the bills during the next half-

[1] Hansard, xxxix. p. 550.

[2] Brougham (1828 A.D.) in Hansard, xviii. p. 127; in the separate
edition of that Speech, p. 65.

year[1]." On poor men and men of moderate means the law operated still more harshly. They had no facilities in obtaining bail; if they did obtain it, they paid in one way or another for the favour; if they did not, they must go to prison.

When, on the other hand, the case against a debtor had once been tried before the Court, the creditor who recovered judgment had no longer the same latitude to obtain satisfaction from his debtor. He might proceed against the debtor's property. Against the freeholds and leaseholds of his debtor he might issue a writ of elegit, but the writ only availed to the extent of one-half of his debtor's land; nor could he sell that half to realize his claim; the most that he could do was to collect the income as tenant by elegit, even if that income were less than the interest on the debt owed to him; and if his debtor was a tenant in tail, he could only collect the income during the life of his debtor. If his debtor possessed any copyholds, he could not touch them, for legal theory forbade that the lord of the manor should have a tenant forced upon him against his will; it made no difference if the lord of the manor waived his right. Against the goods and chattels of his debtor the creditor's ordinary remedy was the writ of *fieri facias*, under which the sheriff seized and sold the debtor's goods. But the writ only applied to such tangible objects as had formed the bulk of man's moveable possessions in the ancient days, many centuries ago, when the writ was first invented. It did not apply to money, " for the quaint reason," as

[1] *Speech of* 1828 A.D., p. 65.

Lord Mansfield considered it, " that money could not be sold, and one was required by the writ to take one's debt out of the produce of the goods sold[1]." Nor did the writ apply to stocks, nor to shares, nor to other securities, nor to debts owed by others to the debtor. It may in fact be said that when the Queen's reign began, three-fourths of the debtor's average personalty, consisting of stock, money and credit, was beyond the reach of his creditor. A debtor might easily arrange his property in such a manner as entirely to defeat his creditors. If a clever man was able but unwilling to pay, he could not be compelled to do so. If a man borrowed a thousand pounds, and the lender obtained judgment for it, the sheriff's officer might come into the debtor's house and might take a table or a desk ; but if he saw the identical thousand pounds lying there, he must leave it ; he touched it at his peril[2].

As if to compensate him, the law allowed the judgment creditor to imprison his debtor by the writ *capias ad satisfaciendum*. If the creditor used this right, he discharged his debtor's property, and had to take the chance of enforcing payment by the pressure of confinement. If the debtor preferred remaining in prison to paying his debts, the creditor's remedies were at an end. There were in 1838 many debtors who were perfectly able to pay their debts, but who were content rather to remain confined[3].

While the creditor's remedies were thus deficient in the most vital points, they were so contrived as to

---

[1] Brougham's *Speech on Law Reform* (1828 A.D.), p. 108.

[2] The Lord Chancellor in Hansard, xxxix. p. 553 (1838 A.D.).

[3] *Ibid.* p. 554.

inflict much incidental injury on third parties. The Statute of Edward I.[1] which provided the writ of elegit had been judicially interpreted to apply to all freeholds which the debtor possessed at the time of the judgment or at any time afterwards, even if he had sold or mortgaged them before the issue of the writ. Judgment debts, in other words, became a lien or charge upon the land. To mitigate the insecurity thus arising to purchasers and mortgagees of land, dockets or books of judgments were established by an Act of William and Mary[2]. This hardly improved matters, for purchasers had at an enormous expense to search the dockets for judgments against any person who had been the owner of any part of the land they intended to buy. The dockets contained names only without any descriptions, and against common names, like Smith, Brown, White, upwards of five hundred judgments were often registered[3].

In 1838 a bill founded in part upon the recommendations of the Real Property Commissioners[4] became law and is known indifferently as the "Judgments Act" or the "Prisoners Act" of 1838[5]. This most important Act abolished arrest on mesne process and greatly extended the creditor's rights against the property of his debtor. It provided that under a writ of elegit the sheriff might deliver execution of *all* lands, including leaseholds and copyholds, of which the debtor or any person in trust[6] for him was seized

---

[1] 13 Ed. I. c. 18.   [2] 4 & 5 W. & M. c. 20.

[3] John Tyrrell, *Evidence etc.*, p. 182.

[4] *First Report*, p. 59.   [5] 1 & 2 Vict. c. 110.

[6] The creditor's remedies had under the Statute of Frauds (29

or possessed at the time of entering up judgment or at any time afterwards. The creditor's tenancy by elegit was extended after the death of a debtor tenant in tail[1], and was also made reasonably complete, for instead of leaving the creditor to gather rents and profits, the Act entitled him to take proceedings in equity for realizing his debt. With regard to personalty, the Act also made a great improvement. It provided that money and bank notes belonging to the judgment debtor, and also debts owing to him and secured by cheque, bill, note, bond, specialty or other security, might be seized by the sheriff for the benefit of the judgment creditor, and that the debtor's stock might be charged by the Court with the payment of the judgment debt[2].

By these provisions the Judgments Act enabled creditors to get at the property of their debtors; but it did little to protect innocent purchasers and mortgagees. On the contrary, the Act expressly provided that a judgment should operate as a charge on the land, and that the writ of elegit should extend to all lands of which the debtor was seized or possessed at the time of the judgment or at any time afterwards. The Act, and two other Acts of 1839 and 1840, also extended the effect of judgments to all decrees and orders of Courts of Equity and Common Law.

Car. II. c. 3, s. 10) been very partial and inadequate against the trust estates of the debtor, and against land over which the debtor had a power of appointment (1 & 2 Vict. c. 110, s. 11).

[1] 1 & 2 Vict. c. 110, s. 13.

[2] 1 & 2 Vict. c. 110, ss. 14 & 15, extended by 3 & 4 Vict. c. 82, s. 1.

Judgments were, however, deprived of their power of affecting purchasers, mortgagees, or other creditors, unless registered against the debtor's name and re-registered every five years in an index provided. This provision did not succeed in removing the inconveniences caused by the lien of judgments. The lien of judgments had, indeed, the advantage of affording a cheap and easy security to creditors, especially by the method of a " warrant of attorney " to enter up judgment against a debtor, which proceeding had the additional advantage of dispensing with the investigation of the debtor's title to his lands. A judgment, again, possessing the quality of binding after-acquired freeholds, creditors often took a judgment by consent as a collateral security, on the chance that the debtor might become possessed of freeholds. Towards the middle of the century, however, as mortgages almost invariably contained powers of sale and other facilities for realizing, judgments fell into disuse as collateral securities. When they *were* so used, it was as a rule by persons who least deserved the favour of the law. Moneylenders, for example, entered up judgments in the hope of catching expectancies under family settlements or wills, and the interest demanded on these occasions was often exorbitantly high, sometimes 50 or 60 per cent. per annum[1]. While its advantages were thus few, the lien of judgments caused enormous expense to purchasers and mortgagees, and often rendered land unsaleable. Whenever a judgment debtor having a large estate wished to sell any portion, however small,

---

[1] *Vide Parl. Pap.* 1864, v. p. 621.

he had to get rid of the judgment, and this was a troublesome and costly process, for the judgment was a lien on *all* his lands, and by the technical rule of law, the judgment could not be released even by deed, until after execution levied. An equally serious expense was incurred by intending purchasers and mortgagees in searching for judgments. The Select Committee on the Judgments Bill of 1864 reported[1] that £80,000 was annually thus spent, and that with all their expense, searches were not always effectual, from the great difficulty of identifying the judgment debtor, especially if he had often changed his abode. The search might also be ineffectual through not being continued up to the last moment; it was the correct practice to search till 4 p.m., when the Registry Office closed, and then to telegraph the result of the search, in order that the transaction might be completed before 11 a.m. next day, when the Registry Office opened again.

To mitigate these real evils, Lord St Leonards in 1860 carried an Act, suggested by the Land Transfer Commission of 1854–7, providing that judgments should not be a lien on the land as against *bonâ fide* purchasers or mortgagees, unless a writ of execution should have been issued and registered before the conveyance or mortgage, and unless the writ were executed within three months after registration. A substantial improvement was thus made, in preventing dormant judgments from remaining an incubus on title, and in preventing the non-execution of writs

---

[1] *Parl. Pap.* 1864, v. p. 620.

issued. Unfortunately, however, the Act required writs of execution to be registered against the creditor's name, and not against the debtor's name, the result of which was to render a double search necessary where a single search had sufficed before. A bill of 1864 proposed a radical cure by abolishing the lien of judgments altogether until the land should have been actually taken and delivered under the writ of execution. The bill was submitted to a Select Committee, which took some evidence and testified to the expense of the existing system of searching and registering judgments. It may be gathered from their Report that judgment debts were a great hindrance to the transfer of realty, even where the creditor was willing to waive his rights in favour of the transferee; that the expense of searching for judgments and writs of execution was so great, that purchasers and mortgagees often preferred to take all risks rather than incur that expense; searches indeed were not made for more than one-tenth of the number of sales and mortgages taking place. The Committee also thought that some injury was done to commercial credit by the publicity of registered judgments[1]. For all these reasons, the Committee approved of the bill, which accordingly passed into law as the Judgments Act of 1864[2]. It provided that no judgment should affect land until the land should have been actually delivered in execution by virtue of a writ of elegit or other lawful authority, and that every writ by which land should have been so delivered should be registered against the *debtor's* name.

[1] *Parl. Pap.* 1864, v. pp. 619, 624. [2] 27 & 28 Vict. c. 112.

For some years the Act operated very well, but
afterwards it was found that notwithstanding the
care with which it had been prepared it was entirely
inadequate for the protection of purchasers and mortgagees; indeed, it took away from the latter the
protection which they had received from the Act of
1860. The trouble arose thus:—Before the Judicature
Act of 1873 the Court of Chancery gave relief to a
judgment creditor only when he was prevented from
using the writ of elegit by the fact that the legal
estate of his debtor's land was vested in some other
person not a simple trustee for the debtor. By the
Judicature Act[1] the Court was enabled to depart from
this rule and to grant a receiver of profits in all cases
where it considered it just or convenient to do so[2]. It
was next held that land was actually "delivered in
execution" when an order had been made for the
appointment of a receiver[3]; and in 1886 it was held[4]
that an order for the appointment of a receiver bound
land in the hands of a purchaser or a mortgagee even
though unregistered, the Court considering that the
Act of 1864 required registration only for the purpose
of obtaining a summary order for sale under the 4th
section of the Act. This decision excited much alarm
among purchasers and mortgagees of land and their
legal advisers, and led to the passing of the Land
Charges, Searches and Registration Act of 1888[5], in-

[1] 36 & 37 Vict. c. 66, s. 5, sub-s. 8.

[2] Cotton, L.J., in xvii. Q.B.D. p. 749.

[3] *Hatton* v. *Haywood*, L.R. 9 Ch. 229.

[4] *Re Pope*, xvii. Q.B.D. 743.

[5] 51 & 52 Vict. c. 51, amended by the Land Charges Act, 1900;
63 & 64 Vict. c. 26, s. 2.

troduced by Lord Hobhouse. This Act has finally
settled the difficulty by providing that every writ or
order affecting land, and every delivery in execution,
shall be void as against purchasers, mortgagees, lessees,
or any transferrees or chargees for valuable consideration,
unless registered in the Office of Land Registry against
the debtor's name.

Other enactments of the Queen's reign have extended
and completed the work begun by the Judgments Act
of 1838 in enabling the judgment creditor to get at the
property of his debtor. Lord Chancellor Cranworth did
not see "why a man who owed him £100, and would
not pay him, should not be obliged to give up the £100
owed him by another man, in satisfaction of his debt[1]";
so he inserted in his Common Law Procedure Act of
1854[2] a section empowering the Court to order that all
debts owed to a judgment debtor might be attached to
answer the judgment. By the Judgments Act of 1864[3],
already mentioned, the creditor's remedy by elegit was
again amplified, the Act providing that a tenant by
elegit under a duly registered writ may summarily
obtain an order for the sale of the debtor's land. Notice
of the sale is given to other judgment creditors, if any,
and the proceeds are distributed amongst them in the
order of their priorities. An enactment of 1861, again,
removed an abuse to which the law of execution had
been liable. Under the then existing law, one creditor,
by levying a timely execution, could monopolize all the

[1] Hansard, cxxx. p. 1342.

[2] 17 & 18 Vict. c. 125, ss. 60, 61, extended by 23 & 24 Vict. c. 126,
ss. 28–31.

[3] 27 & 28 Vict. c. 112, ss. 4, 5.

property of a debtor whose goods were insufficient to pay all his creditors. The injustice of this was apparent, and it also became known that it was a practice among some men of business and capital to set up another in trade, guarding themselves with a warrant of attorney by which they could sell the latter up as soon as his circumstances became embarrassed, to the exclusion of all other creditors. It was therefore enacted by a section of the Bankruptcy Act of 1861[1] (but with respect to trader-debtors only), that execution by the seizure and sale of goods upon a judgment exceeding £50 was an act of bankruptcy, and that the judgment creditor should pay over the proceeds of such sale to the assignee under the bankruptcy, if the debtor were adjudged bankrupt within fourteen days after the sale. The Bankruptcy Acts of 1883 and 1890[2] have made it an act of bankruptcy if the goods of any debtor are seized under process in any Court, or in any civil proceeding in the High Court, and the goods are either sold or held by the sheriff for twenty-one days.

We have now to pass on to the law concerning the creditors of a deceased person, and the distribution of his property among them.

When the Queen's reign commenced, two recent Statutes had removed one of the worst iniquities ever inflicted on creditors by a legislature of landowners. The Statutes[3] referred to had made the land of a deceased debtor liable to his debts. The property, however,—

---

[1] 24 & 25 Vict. c. 134, s. 73.

[2] 46 & 47 Vict. c. 52, s. 4, sub-s. 1 (e); and 53 & 54 Vict. c. 71, s. 1.

[3] 47 Geo. III. c. 74; 3 & 4 Will. IV. c. 104.

personal as well as real—of a deceased debtor was still distributed amongst his creditors in a most capricious order. One rank of creditors was preferred to another for reasons historical rather than meritorious. So long as the property of the debtor deceased was sufficient to pay all his creditors, this caused no greater harm than long-protracted and harassing litigation[1]; but when the property was insufficient, there was the added evil that the most deserving creditors were often those who suffered most in the distribution.

The Crown took precedence over all other creditors, a slight advantage to the public revenue being thus obtained at the cost of much hardship to private creditors. After the Crown came judgment creditors, who were paid in full before any other creditors, a preference corresponding to no relevant distinction between judgment creditors and other creditors. Judgment creditors often became such with the express purpose of gaining priority[2]; and where they were made such by the contentious jurisdiction of the Courts, no reason is apparent why debts which have been contested before a court of law should be preferred to those which are admitted without dispute. The explanation of the preference is of course historical.

Next came creditors by specialty, *i.e.* by covenant, bond, or sealed contract. They were paid in full before any creditors by simple contract were paid at all, although in each case the nature of the obligation was exactly the same. As a general rule, trade creditors did not get bonds executed, but merely bills of ex-

---

[1] *Vide First Report of Real Prop. Comm.* p. 59.

[2] *Vide Parl. Pap.* 1864, v. p. 621.

change or promissory notes, or their credit remained in the shape of a book-credit; on the other hand, members of the debtor's family, or private friends who lent money, got signed and sealed documents. When the debtor died, his friends and relatives, including the trustees of his marriage settlement, came in and were paid in full, while the trade creditors got little or nothing. So again, creditors by specialty in which the heirs were bound (which was most usual) were paid in full out of the realty of the deceased, before other specialty creditors. This preference, arising out of a most trivial difference in the common form of sealed documents, only arose if the deceased debtor had omitted or forgotten to charge his debts on his realty.

The legislation of the Queen's reign has done much, although in an unsystematic and imperfect manner, to remove these venerable freaks of the law. An important Act of 1869[1], due to Hinde Palmer, placed creditors by simple contract on a level with specialty creditors, whether the heirs were bound or not, providing that no debt should be entitled to any priority by reason merely of being a specialty debt. A still more important change was made by the Bankruptcy Act of 1883[2]. Under this Act any creditor of a deceased debtor, whose claim would have been sufficient to support a bankruptcy petition had the debtor been alive, may petition the Court for an order for the administration of the deceased debtor's estate according to the law of bankruptcy; and even after proceedings have been commenced in any Court for the administration of the deceased debtor's estate, the Court may on

[1] 32 & 33 Vict. c. 46.   [2] 46 & 47 Vict. c. 52, s. 125.

the application of any creditor, and on proof that the
estate is insufficient to pay its debts, transfer the
proceedings to the Court exercising jurisdiction in
bankruptcy; and by a later enactment[1], any Court may
so transfer such proceedings, without waiting for the
application of a creditor, whenever it is satisfied that
the estate is unable to pay its debts.

Substantially these provisions have removed the
evils attending the priority of Crown debts and judgment debts; for by the more recent law of bankruptcy[2]
neither judgment debts nor Crown debts have any
priority over simple contract debts.   Substantially,
whenever an estate is not sufficient to pay its debts,
either the creditors or the Court can procure an
equitable administration in bankruptcy.   Solvent estates, however, are still administered with the old
priorities of Crown and judgment debts.   It is to be
regretted, as Mr Cyprian Williams remarks, that the
bankruptcy rules as to the payment of debts have not
been made universally applicable in the administration
of deceased debtors' estates[3].

We now pass to the laws of bankruptcy, which,
next to the laws of business association, constitute the
most important department of the commercial code.
A detailed history of bankruptcy in this country would
not only be a most wearisome task, but would, as Lord
Cairns once declared, be " highly unprofitable in itself."
It has been a history of continual changes, a perpetual
swinging of the pendulum in obedience to the breath

---

[1] 53 & 54 Vict. c. 71, s. 21, sub-s. 2.

[2] 32 & 33 Vict. c. 71, s. 32; 46 & 47 Vict. c. 52, s. 150.

[3] Williams, *Personal Property*, Part II. ch. III.

of public opinion, " each vacillation in turn the subject
of great expectations, and each in turn doomed after
a few years' experience to disappointment and failure."
Since the reign of Henry VIII. we have had bankruptcy
legislation on an average every ten years, and during
the Queen's reign (to say nothing of bills that have
come to grief) on an average every five years[1]. We
shall consequently have to confine ourselves to the
merest outline of the principal changes which have
been made by the bankruptcy legislation of the last
sixty years.

The main legal feature of bankruptcy is the
discharge, by the State, of an insolvent debtor from
his liability to his creditors. The discharge may be
absolute or conditional, total or partial; it has been
known to law in many ages and in many countries,
but in no country to so striking an extent as in
modern England.

The utilitarian basis of bankruptcy is of course to be
found in the consideration that perpetual liability for
the whole of his debt would withdraw from the insolvent
debtor all inducement to thrift and industry; he would
either become a burden on the community, or he would
confine his earnings to the bare limits of the necessities
of subsistence. The discharge of his liabilities, again,
inflicts no injury on his creditors, for they could not in
any case force him to labour productively for their
benefit. This was the view taken in 1840 by the
Royal Commission on Bankruptcy[2]. " The liability

---

[1] *Vide* Lord Cairns in 1868 A.D., Hansard, cxci. p. 2; and Serjeant
Simon (1883 A.D.), Hansard, cclxxii. p. 869.

[2] *Parl. Pap.* 1840, xvi. from p. 9.

of the after-acquired estate," they reported, "though rarely productive to creditors, is apt to paralyze the future exertions of the insolvent, and to throw a gloom over the rest of his days.......The future liability of debtors is in our opinion a most unjust and *impolitic* law; after interrupting a man in his business, taking all his property, imprisoning him until his place in business is occupied, and then turning him out destitute, a proclaimed insolvent, and unworthy of trust, it nevertheless expects him at some future time to acquire property which he is to give up for distribution among his creditors. *The practical result is* that he makes no exertion beyond supplying his daily wants, and too frequently becomes a permanently degraded character; his family are brought up ill; hence society loses and the creditors do not gain." On such considerations the bankruptcy law of England has proceeded in providing for the relief of debtors unable to pay their debts.

The main feature of bankruptcy law being the cancellation of indebtedness, a number of difficult practical problems at once arise. "There is hardly anything," says Mill[1], "on which the economic well-being of mankind depends more than on their being able to trust to each other's engagements, and the preservation of pecuniary integrity is more under the influence of the law, for good and evil, than any other point of public morals." The prospect of relief from debt has an inevitable tendency to encourage fraud, reckless speculation, extravagant living; this tendency may be counteracted by criminal punishment or by

---

[1] *Political Economy*, Bk. v. ch. ix. § 8.

refusing relief to insolvent debtors who cannot show their blamelessness. Besides guarding the morality of trade, the State has to consider how the property presently possessed by an insolvent debtor is to be collected and distributed; whether a debtor shall be allowed to make voluntary and private arrangements with the whole body of his creditors, or whether a public examination shall be compulsory whenever there is an insufficiency of assets, and if voluntary arrangements are permitted, whether they shall be facilitated by empowering a majority of creditors to bind a minority. On all these points the law of England has fluctuated much and often during the last sixty years, and it cannot yet be considered to have attained a condition of stability.

At the present day the principles of the bankruptcy law apply to all persons similarly situated; it was otherwise at the commencement of the Queen's reign. If a merchant prince became insolvent, it was considered to be due to the "inevitable vicissitude of mercantile affairs"; if a retail trader or any other person became insolvent, it was ascribed to extravagance or, at the least, improvidence. In accordance with this distinction, the law of bankruptcy was confined to the merchant with large liabilities which he was unable to meet; it was currently thought that if he remained liable to his debts for the rest of his life, he would never be able to regain his position or to carry on his trade in a manner at once creditable, industrious and profitable to the realm. The bankruptcy law therefore discharged his person and his after-acquired property from all liability. Other debtors, on the other hand,

could be imprisoned by final process at the pleasure of
their creditors, and they could only obtain a discharge
from their liabilities by payment in full. Small traders,
although much less able to recover their position or to
re-acquire property, yet remained subject to a continuing
liability from which wealthier traders were exempted.

The evils of imprisonment by the writ *capias ad
satisfaciendum* are too well-known to readers of *Pick-
wick Papers* to need much telling ; they were vividly
summed up by the Bankruptcy Commissioners of 1840[1].
" When the judgment debtor is imprisoned, his fate is
decided. Cut off from his business, his family, his home,
deprived of the means of honest exertion, shut up in a
gaol, his affairs, if bad before, are now become desperate,
whilst confinement impairs his health, a sense of degradation weighs down his mind, and whilst he is tempted
to raise his sinking spirits by temporary dissipation
amongst depraved associates, he becomes bankrupt in
morals as well as estate."

The lot of non-traders was much alleviated by the
" Prisoners Act " of 1838[2]. This Act enabled a non-
trader debtor actually in prison for debt to obtain
release from confinement by filing a petition to the
" Insolvent Debtors' Court " established by the Act ;
but the debtor's after-acquired property still remained
liable for all his unsatisfied debts. Succeeding Acts[3] of
Parliament extended to non-trader debtors most of the
privileges of the bankruptcy law. By the year 1860,
if non-traders had become insolvent without fraud or

[1] *Parl. Pap.* 1840, xvi. p. 23.

[2] 1 & 2 Vict. c. 110 ; also known as the " Judgments Act."

[3] 7 & 8 Vict. c. 96 ; 10 & 11 Vict. c. 102.

culpable negligence they might obtain a complete discharge from their debts.

The distinction between bankruptcy and insolvency, however, still continued to exist. Of the two, the law of insolvency was superior in affording a more effective power of punishing culpable debtors by a remand to prison. Its great defect was the indiscriminate imprisonment, in the first instance, of all insolvent debtors, whether honest or not; this was found by the Bankruptcy Commission of 1840 to " level the distinction between guilt and misfortune, and to occasion great moral evils by its tendency to subdue that proper degree of pride and honest feeling which is inconsistent with the degradation of imprisonment in a gaol[1]." The same Commission[2] most urgently recommended the abolition of the distinction between traders and non-traders. It was not however till the year 1861 that the inevitable inconvenience of maintaining two separate systems of laws and Courts for debtors in difficulties led to the abolition of that distinction. In that year an Act[3], due to Lord Westbury, subjected all insolvent debtors to the bankruptcy law and abolished the " Insolvent Debtors' Court." The Act did not, however, deprive creditors of their power of imprisoning non-trader debtors; but it enabled a debtor in prison for debt to apply in a summary way for his discharge in bankruptcy; and in case he should not think fit so to apply on his own accord, a sort of gaol-delivery was provided at frequent intervals, the

[1] *Parl. Pap.* 1840, xvi. p. 23.   [2] *Ibid.* p. 10.
[3] 24 & 25 Vict. c. 134.

Bankruptcy Registrars attending the various Debtors' Prisons and liberating the inhabitants *nolentes volentes.*

By these provisions the creditor's power over the person of his debtor had become merely mischievous. It was not even an indirect instrument for compelling payment, since the debtor could not be kept in prison, and it gave rise to a multitude of bankruptcies on the petition of imprisoned debtors who had no assets whatever, whereby much expense was caused without the least utility to creditors[1]. In 1869 the Attorney-General, Sir R. P. Collier, carried an Act abolishing imprisonment for debt. This, the famous Debtors' Act of 1869[2], still allows a debtor to be imprisoned not only when he has been guilty of fraud or of abuses of trust or of contempt of Court, but also when, being a judgment debtor, he has the means to pay and refuses to do so; but this just and reasonable imprisonment is in the discretion of the Court and not of the creditor, it is punitive in nature and does not deprive the creditor of his remedy against the debtor's property. The Act has not only abolished the indiscriminate imprisonment of judgment debtors, but has also deprived the judgment creditor of all power over the person of his debtor.

We have thus seen how the Bankruptcy Law was at length extended to all embarrassed debtors; we shall now transfer our attention to the principles and the provisions themselves of which that law has consisted.

---

[1] Report of Select Committee on Bankruptcy, 1865, *Parl. Pap.* 1865, xii. p. 589. In the year 1862, out of 9663 bankruptcies 6910 were without assets; in the year 1863, 5630 out of 8470.

[2] 32 & 33 Vict. c. 62.

When the Queen's reign began, creditors (except in the London district) had the full and nearly exclusive control of the administration of bankrupt estates, and hardly any provision existed for the punishment by the State of dishonesty or gross negligence on the part of the bankrupt. If the bankrupt fully disclosed his transactions and submitted to the jurisdiction of the Court, even at the last moment and after a most litigious resistance, his misconduct, however flagrant, could not be visited by any direct punishment[1]. The immunity thus enjoyed by bankrupts was all the more remarkable in view of the purpose with which the English law of bankruptcy was originally instituted. That purpose was to benefit *creditors* and to enable them to cope with forms of fraud not dealt with by the ordinary law. Traders were, more than other persons, able to injure the general body of their creditors by fraud, by collusion, by combination with certain of their creditors; this was the reason why, in the reign of Elizabeth, the original severities of the bankruptcy law were confined to traders. The early law of bankruptcy, again, contained no provision for the discharge of the bankrupt's after-acquired property from liability for his unsatisfied debts. An Act of 1706[2] first introduced a "certificate of conformity," by means of which a bankrupt conforming to the law was discharged from all future liability for his past debts; but such a certificate could only be issued with the consent of four-fifths in value of his creditors. Before the Queen's reign, in short, no man's after-acquired

---

[1] *Parl. Pap.* 1840, xvi. p. 7.   [2] 4 & 5 Anne c. 17.

property could be freed from liability for unsatisfied debts without the consent of his creditors. In 1840, however, it was suggested that creditors sometimes withheld their consent vexatiously or from improper motives[1]; and on this ground an Act of 1842[2] directed the Bankruptcy Court to discharge a bankrupt's property from the payment of his debts, if the bankrupt was not fraudulent and had " conformed." The same Act, on the recommendation of the Bankruptcy Commission[3], extended to the whole country a system of official administration of bankrupt estates which had in 1831 been adopted in the London Bankruptcy Court.

The Bankruptcy Act of 1842 worked in every respect most unsatisfactorily. It assured debtors of the immunity of their after-acquired property notwithstanding any degree of reckless misconduct, short of actual fraud, of which they might have been guilty ; and it contributed to cause the mania of speculation which culminated in the commercial panic of 1847. Of the largely increased number of bankruptcies which followed immediately upon the passing of the Act, the statistics[4] showed that by far the greater number arose from " notorious misconduct, gambling, and wildly-absurd speculations." A remedy was attempted in 1849 by an Act of Parliament[5] due to the efforts of Lord Brougham. This Act, besides consolidating the

---

[1] *Parl. Pap.* 1840, xvi. p. 9.   [2] 5 & 6 Vict. c. 112.

[3] *Parl. Pap.* 1840, xvi. p. 26.

[4] Given by J. H. Elliott in *Credit the life of Commerce*, 1845 ; cited by Mill, *Political Economy*, Bk. v. ch. ix. § 8.

[5] 12 & 13 Vict. c. 106.

law of bankruptcy, introduced a classification of certificates of conformity into "good," "bad" and "indifferent,"
so as to enable the Court to reward appropriately all
sorts of conduct.

Equally unsatisfactory was the officialism introduced
by the Bankruptcy Act of 1842[1]. It had been thought
that creditors would place reliance in an "Official
Assignee" appointed by the Bankruptcy Court, but
that Court found it from the first impossible to exercise
proper supervision either over the appointment of the
Official Assignees or over the performance of their
duties. As time went on, the Court became more
and more negligent. Appointments were obtained by
notorious jobbery, and the Official Assignee was allowed to do what he thought proper with the funds;
he kept the money in his own hands without being
called to account, and in one or two cases there was
gross peculation[2].

General dissatisfaction was felt with the bankruptcy
law, and a desire grew up, not of entirely abolishing
that law, but of reducing to a minimum its officialism
and of doing away with the *quantum* of interference
—little though it was—which the bankruptcy law
exerted in the interests of public morality, on the
freedom of bargaining between debtors and creditors.
It was currently declared that the sole object of
bankruptcy law was to *get at* a debtor's property and
distribute it among his creditors; that when a debtor
was unable to pay, the first and chief need was to
secure an immediate arrangement between him and

[1] 5 & 6 Vict. c. 112.   [2] *Vide* in Hansard, CCLXXII. p. 826.

his creditors; that when a financial shipwreck took place, the duty of the State was merely to protect the salvage, not to examine into the causes of the shipwreck or to attempt diminishing the number of· wrecks for the future; that the State, in short, had nothing to do with commercial morality.

These short-sighted views, born of the impatient enthusiasm of trade, were widely circulated by the Chambers of Commerce and by their sympathisers in Parliament[1]. A Royal Commission appointed in 1853 made proposals which were in 1859 embodied in a Bill by Lord Chancellor Campbell. The Bill proposed greatly to extend the existing facilities for private arrangements and compositions between debtors and their creditors. Such arrangements and compositions had been first introduced by the Bankruptcy Act of 1825[2], but that Act had required the consent of nine-tenths of the creditors to any deed of arrangement. The Bankruptcy Act of 1849 had somewhat relaxed this requirement, and deeds of arrangement had grown more numerous. Lord Campbell proposed in 1859 to enable every insolvent debtor by arrangement with a majority in number and three-fourths in value of his creditors, to bind a minority of them to a composition or any other scheme which the majority might agree to. Lord Campbell's measure was stopped by the dissolution of Parliament, but it was carried two years later by Lord Westbury, in a section of the Bankruptcy Act

[1] *Vide* e.g. in Hansard, cxcvii. p. 1404; cxcv. from p. 142; cxci. from p. 1; and in *Parl. Pap.* 1852–3, vol. xxii.; *ibid.* 1864, vol. v. from p. 1; *ibid.* 1865, vol. xii. from p. 589.

[2] 6 Geo. IV. c. 16.

of 1861[1]. The same Act, following the tide of public opinion, greatly reduced the powers and functions of the official assignees, and abolished the graduated classes of bankruptcy certificates introduced in 1849, substituting for them a single " order of discharge."

The Bankruptcy Act of 1861[2] worked as badly as its predecessors. The increase of speculation, luxury and insolvency[3] by which it was immediately followed was attributed not to the absence of public examination and the immunity of culpable insolvents, but to the continued existence of Official Assignees (shorn though they were of their powers), and to other superficial circumstances. In 1864 and 1865 a Select Committee of the House of Commons was appointed " to inquire into the operation of the Bankruptcy Act of 1861." After examining a crowd of witnesses, they recommended[4] the total abolition of Official Assignees. This and other proposals of the Committee were substantially adopted in the Bankruptcy Act of 1869[5]. Official Assignees were abolished and the fullest power was given to creditors to make arrangements with insolvent debtors before the commencement of bankruptcy proceedings, and even to stop such proceedings and make arrangements at any time before the final adjudication of bankruptcy[6]. The aim of the Bankruptcy Act of 1869 was described by Lord Chancellor

---

[1] 24 & 25 Vict. c. 134, s. 192. [2] *Ibid.* c. 134.

[3] In 1862, 635 deeds of arrangement were registered ; in 1866 no less than 6912.

[4] *Parl. Pap.* 1864, vol. v. from p. 1 ; *ibid.* 1865, vol. xii. from p. 591.

[5] 32 & 33 Vict. c. 71.

[6] 32 & 33 Vict. c. 71, ss. 125, 126.

Hatherley as being " to secure a man's assets, as soon as possible after he is known to be in a hopeless condition, for the equal benefit of his creditors." " Its object," he declared, " was to encourage a man to come forward as soon as he discovered he was insolvent, and give up his property to his creditors"; and Lord Cairns proclaimed its principle to be " that creditors should be made, as far as possible, masters of their own business; in other words, there should be a maximum of power in the creditors and a minimum of interference on the part of the Court[1]." It was probably on account of the same principle of *laisser faire* that the Act refused to discourage speculation and extravagance. The only thing that it did in that direction was to provide that if a debtor should actually have been made a bankrupt by his creditors, his after-acquired property should remain bound till he had paid ten shillings in the pound, unless his creditors consented to its earlier discharge.

It is generally agreed that the Bankruptcy Act of 1869 was a more disastrous failure than any previous Bankruptcy Act. The institution of Bankruptcy as an entirely optional proceeding, and the facilitation of private arrangement, which were the chief features of the Act, were also its worst faults; they gave rise to every description of fraud and abuse. As Mr Chamberlain has profoundly observed, the gravest vices of the Act flowed from the assumptions underlying it, " that insolvency was a matter which solely concerned the creditors in each particular case, and that the creditors

[1] Hansard (1869), cxcvii. pp. 1404, 1407, 1413.

could and would not only look after their own interests,
but could and would also protect the interests of the
public, which were sometimes quite different from and
inconsistent with their own[1]." The interests of creditors
were, and are, generally too minute and too divided to
allow of anything like complete and organized self-
protection by the creditors themselves ; men of business
were generally utterly careless, and only too ready to
write off their bad debts at once, especially under a
system which, so far from giving them any practical
assistance, invited them to throw good money after bad
and undertake a public duty at their private cost[2].
Traders indeed declared themselves "no more likely to
attend to the business of administering bankrupts'
estates than to carry their own parcels." If creditors
did not find it worth their while to undertake these
duties on their own account, still less did they think it
worth their while to undertake them on behalf of the
public. The interests of the public and the interests
of creditors were often adverse to each other. The
friends of an insolvent debtor might offer a larger
composition than the insolvent estate could pay, in
order to avoid exposure; and creditors, being only
human, often compounded for the misconduct or con-
doned the negligence or the extravagance of the

[1] Hansard, CCLX. p. 1062 (1881 A.D.). *Vide* also Report of Select
Committee on Bankruptcy, *Parl. Pap.* 1880, vol. VIII. from p. 213.

[2] *Vide* Lord Esher, M.R. in Ex parte Reed, 17 Q.B.D. 250; also
the Report for 1875 of the Controller-General, quoted in Hansard
(1881 A.D.), CCLX. p. 1062; and the Memorial presented in 1880 by the
Bankers and Merchants of London to Lord Beaconsfield; quoted in
Hansard, CCLX. p. 1058.

debtor[1]. In a great many cases, too, a creditor might desire to continue business relations with the insolvent, and would therefore be disposed to take a favourable view of his conduct and to avoid inquiry. Experience showed, in short, the futility of relying upon creditors to expose " misconduct, which in the plain interests of public morality and commercial policy, should be dealt with not as a private matter but by a public Court or Judge[2]." In other words, *laisser faire* had failed as a principle of bankruptcy.

The Bankruptcy Act of 1869 contained, as we have seen, the most inadequate provision for punishing the misconduct of insolvents, however grievous; but in practice even such punishment as the Act provided was as a rule entirely inapplicable, being easily evaded by the private arrangements which the Act fostered. As soon as the Act came into operation, there was an ominous increase in the number of liquidations and compositions. In the succeeding decade the annual number of insolvency proceedings increased from 5002 to 13132, the annual liabilities from seventeen million to twenty-nine million pounds. During the same period, the number of bankruptcies proper *decreased* from 1351 to 1156, while the number of liquidations and compositions, altogether independent of judicial authority, *increased* from 3651 to 11976. Only 7 per cent. of all the cases of insolvency were subject to public control, while the other 93 per cent. were left without any State-supervision, without any provision for an independent or impartial examination into the

---

[1] *Vide* Lord Esher, M.R. in Ex parte Reed, 17 Q.B.D. 250.

[2] Bankers' *Memorial, loc. cit.*

causes of the insolvency and the conduct of the insolvent. Liquidations gave rise to many peculiar frauds
and abuses. Voting by proxy being permitted, the
proceedings were often wholly arranged at the discretion
of a single solicitor who had obtained the required
majority of creditors' proxies, and who could thus vote
himself trustee, settle his own remuneration, nominate
his own Committee of Inspection (frequently nominat-
ing sham or collusive creditors) and impose any
arrangement he pleased on a dissenting minority
of *bonâ fide* creditors[1].

So intolerable was the nuisance felt to be, that
between the years 1870 and 1883 no fewer than twenty
Bills, of which eight were Government Bills, were
brought in for amending the Bankruptcy Act of 1869.
A Select Committee of 1880 reported that "the
principal defect in the working of the Act was to
be found in the facilities for fraud which resulted from
the practice of liquidation and composition[2]"; and they
proposed several salutary changes which, to cut the
story short, found their way into the Bankruptcy Act
of 1883.

This Act is now the governing Bankruptcy Act[3].
It sought to profit by past experience, and totally
reversed the policy of the bankruptcy law as contained
in the Act of 1869. The main principle upon which
it is based has been unmistakeably proclaimed by its

---

[1] *Vide* Mr Chamberlain's speeches in introducing the Bankruptcy
Bills of 1881 and 1883. Hansard, CCLX. p. 1060; CCLXXVII. p. 816;
Bankers' *Memorial*, *loc. cit.*; and *Parl. Pap.* 1880, VIII. p. 211.

[2] *Parl. Pap.* 1880, VIII. from p. 211.

[3] 46 & 47 Vict. c. 52.

promoters in Parliament. The State has not only
to protect the salvage of a financial shipwreck but has
also to inquire into its causes, and take prospective
steps for diminishing the number of such wrecks. As
Mill would have said, " it is the business of the law
to prevent wrongdoing, and not simply to patch up
the consequences of it when it has been committed."
Insolvency is not necessarily a crime, but it indicates
a condition of things which throws on the insolvent the
burden of proving that he should not be held responsible for the injury done to his creditors[1]. In
pursuance of this principle the Act lays down most
distinctly that without the free consent of all his
creditors no man shall be relieved from his liabilities
until a public examination has first taken place into
the causes and circumstances of his indebtedness. No
composition or scheme of arrangement can be made
to bind a single dissenting creditor unless and until
bankruptcy proceedings have been taken up to the
stage of the public examination of the insolvent at the
first meeting of creditors; and the Court can refuse to
ratify any arrangement not only if it considers that it
would be detrimental to the creditors generally, but
also if the debtor has been found guilty of acts which
would deprive him of the right to discharge if made
bankrupt, or if the arrangement appears prejudicial to
the morality of trade[2].

The inevitable public inquiry is conducted by a

[1] *Vide* Mr Chamberlain in Hansard, CCLXXVII. p. 817 et seqq.; Lord
Chancellor Selborne, Hansard, CCLXXXIII. p. 940 ; and Mill, *Political
Economy*, Bk. v. ch. IX. § 8.

[2] *Vide* Esher, M.R. in Ex parte Reed, 17 Q.B.D. 250.

public officer, the Official Receiver. The Official Receiver is an officer of the Court, and therefore (like the Official Assignee of bygone days) under the control of the Court; but (unlike him) the Official Receiver is further responsible to the Board of Trade, by whom he is appointed and directed. The Official Receiver investigates the conduct of the insolvent and the causes which have led to his insolvency, conducts the examination before the Court, and reports to the Court when the question of discharging a bankrupt is considered. The officialism of the Act extends to the administration of bankrupt estates, *i.e.* to the collection, realization and distribution of the bankrupt's property; but here also its officialism differs materially from that of the Official Assignee of the earlier part of the Queen's reign. The creditors themselves, through their own trustee, collect and distribute the bankrupt's assets, under the supervision of the Official Receiver, the interference of the latter being limited to what is necessary for protecting the minority of creditors, and for securing honest dealing on the part of everyone concerned in the administration of the estate. The system of checks and balances is carried still further. The trustee for the creditors is required to keep proper books of account open to the inspection both of the Board of Trade and of the creditors' committee of inspection; he is also required to send an annual statement of his progress to the Board of Trade.

The Act, lastly, has made ample provision for meting out appropriate justice to erring debtors; the discharge of a bankrupt's after-acquired property is no longer a matter of course by any means. It is in the power of

the Court to make various conditions as to the after-
acquired property in discharging a bankrupt, and the
Court is specially directed by the Act to refuse discharge whenever the bankrupt has committed any
misdemeanour or felony in connection with his bankruptcy. If the bankrupt has not assets enough to pay
his creditors ten shillings in the pound, the burden of
proof lies on him to show that this is due to circumstances for which he cannot justly be held responsible;
and if he has on a prior occasion been bankrupt or made
an arrangement with his creditors, the Court may refuse
to discharge him, or may suspend his discharge till he
has paid ten shillings in the pound, or may make his
after-acquired property *liable to all or part of the debts
provable in the bankruptcy*[1]. The Act has moreover
provided bankrupts with a powerful inducement to
fulfil such conditions-previous to their discharge, by
making it a criminal offence for an undischarged bankrupt to obtain credit to the extent of twenty pounds
without stating that he is an undischarged bankrupt.
Under the Act of 1869, bankrupts had not been very
anxious to obtain their discharge; it appears to have
been a matter of perfect indifference to a bankrupt
whether he was discharged or not; in the year 1881, out
of 5207 bankrupts only 606 applied for their discharge[2].
It seems, however, that the Bankruptcy Act of 1883
has not altogether put an end to the inertia of undischarged bankrupts[3].

---

[1] 46 & 47 Vict. c. 52, ss. 31, 163–7 ; 53 & 54 Vict. c. 71, s. 8.

[2] Controller's Report for that year, quoted by Mr Chamberlain in
Hansard, CCLXXII. p. 816.

[3] *Vide* Hansard (1893 A.D.), XL. p. 1131.

One result of the stringent inquisitions and incorruptible officialism of the Act has been very similar to that which, though from opposite causes, followed the Bankruptcy Act of 1869 ; viz., a great decrease in the number of bankruptcies and a great increase in the number of deeds of assignment for the benefits of creditors generally. Such assignments the Act has not interfered with, provided that all the creditors agree to the assignment. The whole body of creditors may make what terms they please ; they may forgive the insolvent his entire debt. The requirement of a public inquiry only arising with the necessity of binding a dissenting creditor, assignments to which all agree may still be made extra-judicially, nor is it likely that the compulsory examination of the Act will ever be extended to such assignments; by the Deeds of Arrangement Act of 1887[1], however, some publicity has been secured to such assignments ; provision has been made for their public registration, on pain of nullity.

We have in conclusion to deal with the contractual securities over moveable and immoveable property, which have in recent times attracted a good deal of attention.

Besides the general liability of property for the debts of its owner, most codes of law enable an owner of property while remaining in possession to make a determinate portion or the whole of it liable for some particular debt owed to some particular creditor. So long as this right is used for its legitimate object of

[1] 50 & 51 Vict. c. 87.

procuring an advance of money, it is on the whole a useful incident of ownership. The temporary necessities of the owner are relieved, and yet he retains possession and enjoyment of his property until default in repayment; on such default, the claim of the secured creditor to the pledged property is recognized as having priority over the claims of other creditors, and justly so, for the security formed part of the consideration for his advance. The great disadvantage of contractual securities unaccompanied with change of possession lies in the opening which they afford to fraud, the ease with which they may be diverted from their legitimate object, and the extreme difficulty of detecting sinister dealings with them. The owner remaining in possession may gain a " false and delusive credit, and may obtain money from innocent parties on the hypothesis of his being the owner of that which in fact belongs to his creditor[1]." With regard to real property this danger has been obviated (though clumsily and imperfectly enough) by the conveyancing regulation which gives to the mortgagee the possession of the title-deeds. When personal property, on the other hand, is pledged without change of possession (which is one of the commonest forms of commercial security), there is absolutely nothing to indicate the fact to the external world. The expediency of recognizing the validity of such pledges has consequently been felt to be extremely questionable whenever they cease to be genuinely employed for procuring advances of money. The execution of a bill of sale in consideration of a *past*

[1] *Vide* 3 Russ. 1 (*Dearle* v. *Hall*).

indebtedness is at best a preference of one creditor to others with equal claims, and is usually also a fraudulent or a collusive transaction. The Associated Chambers of Commerce have themselves put on record, as the result of their experience, " that the operation of bills of sale is in the majority of cases fraudulent and injurious to the trading community, besides being the worst form of preferential security."

Against these mischiefs the law of England formerly carried on an unequal contest by means of the Statute of Frauds and the " possession order or disposition " clauses of the Bankruptcy Law. At Common Law[1] a man might take a security upon goods without taking possession, and when an execution was issued against the person in possession of the goods, " the man might suddenly come forward and claim that he had a security on the goods, but had left them in the possession of the debtor." Under the Statute of Frauds a rule became established that the not taking possession was evidence to go to the jury of fraud, but it was inconclusive evidence. Out of this two serious evils arose. If the affair was really a sham, " there was a great quantity of perjury, of fighting, and of expense before it was proved to be so "; if it was an honest transaction " there was apt to be much perjury and great expense before it was decided." In the year 1854 it was thought desirable to put a stop to this, and Parliament entered on a complicated campaign against the astuteness of moneylenders. The Bills of Sale Act of 1854, after reciting that frauds were frequently committed on

[1] Lord Blackburn in *Cookson* v. *Swire*, 9 App. Cas. 664.

creditors by secret bills of sale of personal chattels, whereby persons were enabled to keep up the appearance of being in good circumstances and possessed of property, and the grantees of the bills of sale had the power of taking possession of the property of such persons to the exclusion of the rest of their creditors,— required bills of sale to be registered[1] in the Court of Queen's Bench within twenty-one days of their making[2].

The publicity thus secured to bills of sale somewhat lessened the " false and delusive credit " derivable from the possession of chattels pledged to others, but did not prevent bills of sale from being more often than not fraudulent and collusive transactions; it was as easy to register a fraudulent as a genuine bill of sale. A dodge was moreover discovered by which valid bills of sale might be given without incurring the publicity of registration at all ; under the Bills of Sale Act, 1854, bills of sale had to be registered within twenty-one days of their making, but they were perfectly valid in the intervening time, and a practice arose of renewing bills of sale from time to time before the expiration of the twenty-one days, thus escaping registration altogether.

An Act[3] was accordingly passed in 1878, extending the meaning of the term "bill of sale," providing for the attestation and registration of bills of sale within

[1] 17 & 18 Vict. c. 36.

[2] The registration was rendered more effective by an Act of 1866 (St. 29 & 30 Vict. c. 96), which provided for its renewal every five years.

[3] 41 & 42 Vict. c. 31.

seven days after their making, and making void all renewals of bills of sale within the intervening period. The twentieth section of the same Act[1] provided that the chattels comprised in a registered bill of sale should not be deemed to be in the "possession, order or disposition" (within the meaning of the bankruptcy law) of the grantor. This provision was designed in the interests of trade, and had the approval of all the Chambers of Commerce in the country; but it was soon found to have placed a most effective premium on fraud and collusion, and to operate most disadvantageously to the general body of a man's creditors, however advantageous it might be to a particular one of them[2]. The yearly number of bills of sale at once grew by leaps and bounds. In 1878 there were 19,596 bills of sale registered; in the following year 49,623, most of them fraudulent preferences[3]. The number was again much larger in 1880, partly because of the agricultural depression of that year, and the increase was especially noticeable in bills of sale for small sums, given by artizans and agricultural labourers[4]. Complaints arose from all sides, and in the year 1881 a Select Committee was appointed to consider the subject and examine witnesses. The Lord Chancellor in the same year issued a circular to judges and registrars of County Courts, interrogating them about the operation of the Bills of Sale Act of 1878[5]. From the evidence

[1] 41 & 42 Vict. c. 31, s. 20.

[2] *Vide Parl. Pap.* 1881, VIII. p. 83.

[3] *Ibid.* LXXXIII. p. 1.

[4] *Ibid.* The number of bills of sale for sums under £20 was in 1878, 2308; in 1880, 13978.

[5] *Parl. Pap.* 1881, LXXVI. pp. 1–62.

thus collected, it was plain that almost all bills of sale were fraudulent and unreasonable preferences of one creditor among many, especially such bills as (under the ruling of the House of Lords in *Holroyd* v. *Marshall*) bound the after-acquired property of the grantor[1].

So great was the evil, that the Select Committee seriously considered the question of totally abolishing bills of sale. On reflection, however, they felt that they could not properly deny one man the right to raise money on personalty, while they allowed another to raise it on realty ; it seemed right to them on the whole that a man should have the power of pledging his property whether personal or real, in order to relieve himself from temporary pressure. They decided therefore that bills of sale should continue to be re-cognized by our law, but that as many restrictions as possible should be placed on them in order to prevent fraudulent transactions and protect honest creditors. With this object they recommended that the twentieth section of the Bills of Sale Act of 1878 should be repealed, and that the judiciary rule of *Holroyd* v. *Marshall* should be altered so as to exclude future property from bills of sale[2].

The evidence collected by the Lord Chancellor and the Select Committee threw light on another evil more sensational if not of more real importance. The bills

---

[1] *Holroyd* v. *Marshall*, 10 Clarke, H.L.C. 191 (1861 A.D.). The witnesses variously estimated that 80 to 99 per cent. of the bills of sale registered were fraudulent. *Parl. Pap.* 1881, VIII. p. 75, and LXXVI. p. 66.

[2] *Parl. Pap.* 1881, VIII. from p. 1.

of sale taken by moneylenders for small sums of money were found to be most oppressive, the interest exacted being often outrageous. It was quite a common thing to find bills of sale given by artizans and agricultural labourers for sums of two pounds and upwards, enabling the grantee to take everything which the grantor possessed, *not* excepting his bedding, clothing and tools. The rate of interest usually ranged between seventy and ninety per cent., and in one admitted case it was four hundred per cent. The printed forms circulated by the lowest and most unscrupulous class of moneylenders contained lists of conditions scarcely possible of fulfilment, and forming a series of ingenious traps for poor and ignorant borrowers. The commonest and most successful artifice, according to Serjeant Petersdorff[1], was for the lender to profess to advance, say, £100 for twelve months, to be repayable by equal quarterly or monthly instalments. When the money was advanced, £20 or £25 was generally deducted for expenses, and 40 or 50 per cent. interest was bargained for. There was always an express stipulation that on non-payment of the first or any subsequent instalment the whole amount should become due together with the year's interest at the stipulated rate, making the amount for which seizure and sale was made £140 or £150 instead of £8. 6s. 8d., if it was for the first monthly instalment. Usually the borrower was beguiled into a soothing belief that exact punctuality would not be insisted upon; hence the seizures were frequently made for the first instalment, and everything

---

[1] *Parl. Pap.* 1881, LXXVI. p. 83.

comprised in the bill of 'sale ruthlessly sold at a sham
auction. The Select Committee of 1881 accordingly
came to the conclusion that it would be an advantage
to smaller borrowers if they were prevented entirely
from borrowing on bills of sale ; and proposed that bills
of sale for less than fifty pounds should be made void
for all purposes.

All the recommendations of the Committee were
in substance accepted by an Act of 1882[1], amending
the Act of 1878. The Bills of Sale Act of 1882
applies only to bills of sale or other documents given
by way of security for the payment of money. It
repeals the twentieth section of the Act of 1878, thus
restoring the chattels comprised within a registered
bill of sale to the " possession, order or disposition "
of the grantor; it requires that the chattels comprised
in a bill of sale be actually owned by the grantor ; it
provides a statutory form for bills of sale ; it renders
void all bills of sale for sums under £30 ; it mitigates
the lot of the grantor of a bill of sale by entitling him
to appeal to the Court on seizure of his property, and
by strictly limiting the allowable conditions of seizure
and sale.

We now pass on to real securities. Much has
already been said incidentally about mortgages, about
some of their conveyancing aspects, and about the
devolution of a deceased mortgagee's estate; it remains
to give a brief account of the legislative measures and
projects affecting them more exclusively. Mortgages
are liable, though in a less degree, to dangers similar

[1] 45 & 46 Vict. c. 43.

to those of bills of sale. A good abstract of title and
the possession of the title-deeds afford safeguards with
which a mortgagee-at-law is as a rule perfectly content.
For this reason, and perhaps also because of the resistance of the landed class, and because the registration
of mortgages has generally been included in wider
schemes of registration, there is as yet no compulsory
registration of mortgages corresponding to the publicity
of bills of sale. As soon, however, as the safeguard of
the possession of the title-deeds is withdrawn, a mortgage is a security fully as unreliable as a bill of sale
formerly was. The possession of the title-deeds is
impossible almost as often as not. It is impossible,
for example, in every case where the same land serves
as a security to several creditors. It would seem just
and equitable in such a case that the creditors should
be entitled to satisfaction according to the priority of
their advances, or, at least, according to the priority
of their securities in point of time. In England, however, the peculiar jural form which mortgages have
assumed, together with the dual system of law and
equity, have prevented so simple an arrangement.
The doctrines of tacking and of the consolidation of
securities, which enter into the English arrangement,
are not indeed without advantages; but the advantages
are outweighed by serious drawbacks.

The doctrine of tacking, for example, enables a first
mortgagee to make further advances with safety, and
has thus rendered possible the system of progressive
loans to builders, and many similar practices of great
utility. This advantage, however, is obtained at the
expense of puisne incumbrancers. A second mortgagee

may find his security entirely destroyed through a further advance made by the first mortgagee ; he may, notwithstanding notice given by him to the first mortgagee, find his security destroyed also by a transfer from the first to the third mortgagee[1]. He may thus suffer serious loss through no fault of his own, and through no lack of care and caution other than that of having " meddled with an equity of redemption " at all. The policy of the law might conceivably have been to discourage all mortgages other than first mortgages, that is to say, to limit to a single creditor the security derivable from land. As this, however, is certainly not the policy of the English law, the position of a puisne mortgagee appears to be one of unmerited and irrational misfortune. The right of consolidating securities, again, is of great advantage to the mortgagee-at-law, but causes much inconvenience both to later mortgagees and to purchasers of mortgaged estates. A purchaser of a mortgaged estate may find himself obliged to redeem other estates besides the one purchased by him ; and this is one of the reasons why it is so often impossible to sell a mortgaged estate on anything like reasonable terms.

Both tacking and consolidation place owners of land in a position of great difficulty by making it almost impossible for them to raise money on second mortgages in all cases where the first mortgagee, for one reason or another, refuses a further advance. In other respects also the mortgager is most unfavourably situated. All the difficulties attending the transfer of

[1] *Goddard* v. *Complin* (1 Ch. Ca. 119) ; *Marsh* v. *Lee* (2 Ventris, 337).

land, already described, are present to a still greater
degree in the case of mortgages. There are in mortgages no stipulations dispensing with the full rigour of
proof of title. The mortgager, being in want of money
and being occasionally in the hands of the mortgagee,
is not in a condition to make special terms, and often
suffers grievously both in the matter of delay and of
expense[1]. Mortgages, too, are transactions occurring
far more frequently than purchases of land ; it was
estimated in 1862 that the proportion of mortgages to
purchases was as nine or ten to one[2]. Part of the
expense of mortgages is no doubt inevitable, but much
of it is due to the present long arrangement of conveyance with conditions, provisoes for redemption,
powers of sale and other auxiliary stipulations, followed
ultimately by a reconveyance. Many proposals have
been made for the substitution of a simpler proceeding.
Joshua Williams' plan was to render valid " a simple
charge on the land of principal and interest, with all
necessary remedies, including a power to sell and convey
the fee simple," and then to " prohibit the conveyance
of the legal estate to any person simply for the purpose
of securing the payment of money lent[3]." The suggestion was adopted by the Royal Commission of
1854–7[4] but without any practical result. In 1879 " Mr
Osborne Morgan's Committee " again vainly urged that
legal mortgages and deeds of reconveyance should be
abolished by giving to the holder of a simple charge on

[1] Joshua Williams on *The Transfer of Land* (1862), p. 34.

[2] *Op. cit.* p. 35.

[3] *The Transfer of Land*, p. 36.

[4] *Parl. Pap.* 1857, vol. xviii. p. 298.

land all the remedies possessed by the holder of a legal mortgage, the charge determining *ipso facto* on the satisfaction of the debt[1]. Their chairman calculated that such a change would effect a saving of several millions a year[2].

The Land Transfer Commission of 1854–1857 proposed the abolition of tacking and of consolidation, and in the year 1874 tacking was abolished by the Vendor and Purchaser Act[3]. The Act provided that no priority or protection should be given to any interest in land by reason of such interest being protected by or tacked to any legal estate. It was soon found, however, that the change was premature. So far from remedying the inconveniences of equities of redemption, the Act extended those inconveniences to mortgages of the legal estate, and made it impossible for a first mortgagee (though without notice of any subsequent incumbrance) safely to make further advances. The enactment was therefore retrospectively repealed in the following year by a section of the Land Transfer Act[4].

The Conveyancing Bill of 1881 proposed to abolish entirely the consolidation of securities. Afterwards, however, a doubt was felt whether the parties to a mortgage could possibly be prevented from introducing the right in the shape of an express contract; and so the Conveyancing Act of 1881 merely abolished the right of consolidation *unless* a contrary intention were

[1] *Parl. Pap.* 1879, vol. XI. pp. xii, xiii.
[2] Osborne Morgan, *Land Law Reform,* p. 16.
[3] 37 & 38 Vict. c. 78, s. 7.
[4] 38 & 39 Vict. c. 87, s. 129.

expressed in the mortgage deeds or in one of them. The Act has not done much to remove consolidation from the current practice. Provisions to exclude the Act are frequently inserted in deeds, for in most mortgages the mortgagee has a preponderating voice with regard to minor details[1].

Apparently, then, it is impossible to abolish tacking and consolidation so long as no means are provided for ascertaining the existence of incumbrances on land. It is hoped, however, that the compulsory Registration of Titles will render their abolition easy ; in Yorkshire, at any rate, tacking was expressly abolished by the Yorkshire Registries Act[2] of 1884, and the provision appears to operate effectually.

[1] *Vide Report of Bar Committee*, 25 March 1886, p. 78.
[2] 47 & 48 Vict. c. 54.

INDEX.

Agricultural Holdings Acts, 98, 100
Agricultural Labourers, 34, 38
Allotments, 104
Ancient Demesne, 80
Artistic Copyright, 154–7

Bankruptcy, 203–22
Bills of Exchange, 187
Bills of Sale, 224–9
Borough-English, 81

Certificates of Conformity, 212
Charitable Uses, 71–6
Codification, 185–8
Commandite Partnership, 176–85
Companies, *see* Corporations *and* Joint-stock Companies
Compensation for Improvements, 96, 101
Consolidation of Securities, 231–3
Construction of Wills, 8, 108–11
Conveyancing Act of 1881, 52
Copyholds, 82–91
Copyright, 126, 143–58
Corporations, 161–2
Courts of Probate, 113–15

Debts, 188–203
Deeds, 6, 8, 19
Deeds of Arrangement Act 1887, 222
Distress, 97, 99, 101
Dower, 3, 10

Enfranchisement of Copyholds, 88, 90
Entails, *see* Settlements
Estates Tail, 85–6

Feoffments, 16
Fieri facias, 191
Fixtures, 98, 101
Foreign Inventions, 141

Gavelkind, 80
Grand Serjeanty, 80
Ground Game Act, 102

Heriots, 83

Imprisonment of Debtors, 192, 207, 209
Improvement of Land Acts, 58
Insolvency, 207–8
Intestate's Estates Act, 124

Joint-stock Companies, 163–76
Judgments, 8, 194–9
Judgments Act of 1838, 193, 207

Land Question, 29, 32, 39, 93–5
Land Transfer Act of 1875, 43, 45, 48
Land Transfer Act of 1897, 70
Leasehold Tenants, 34, 36, 93–101
Locke King's Act, 124
Lord St Leonards' Act, 26
Lord Westbury's Act, 25, 41

Mesne Process, 190
Mortgages, 47, 53, 229–34

Notices to quit, 96

Obstructive Patents, 130
Official Assignee, 212

Partnerships, 162–86
Patents, 126–43
Peasant ownership, 37
Powers of appointment, 27, 60
Primogeniture, 120–4
Priorities of Debts, 200–3
Probate of Wills, 113–5, 117–8

Real Actions, 10

Real Property Act of 1845, 16
Realty representatives, 116, 119–20
Registration of Assurances, 11–16, 22, 49
Registration of Judgments, 195–9
Registration of Title, 23–6, 41, 43, 48, 69
Royalty-system, 147
Rural system of England, 43

Sale of Goods Act of 1893, 187
Satisfied Terms, 4, 18
Searches, 8
Settled Land Acts, 54, 59, 60–3, 65
Settlements, 35, 46, 55, 59, 63, 64, 66, 67–9
Solicitors' Charges, 50
Spiritual Tenures, 79
Statutes of Limitation, 3, 10, 44

Tacking, 230, 233
Tenure, 77
Tenures of Land in Europe, 33
Timber and Mines on Copyholds, 85
Tithes, 103
Trademarks, 158–60

Wills, 105–13

For EU product safety concerns, contact us at Calle de José Abascal, 56–1°, 28003 Madrid, Spain or eugpsr@cambridge.org.

www.ingramcontent.com/pod-product-compliance
Ingram Content Group UK Ltd.
Pitfield, Milton Keynes, MK11 3LW, UK
UKHW012328130625
459647UK00009B/145